GROWING UP IN 'LITTLE ITALY'

By

BILL ANDERSON

"Remember, boy, onna' the rose they gon' be some thorn".

Words of wisdom spoken to me by my Grandfather when I was a boy.

Copyright 2017

All rights reserved

INTRODUCTION

I was indeed privileged to grow up in the little town of Krebs in Southeastern Oklahoma. It has now become known as Oklahoma's 'Little Italy'. The above monument was dedicated in the mid 1990's, over 100 years after this terrible coal mining disaster. This explosion which occurred in 1892 proved to be the worst in Oklahoma, and one of the worst in United States history of coal mining. It occurred only a few blocks from my Grandparents' home. Luckily, my Grandfather had not arrived here from Italy. Otherwise he, too, may have been one of the victims. The above photo shows the building which covered the

INTRODUCTION

mine shaft. Below the photo is shown a partial list of some of the victims. During these early times, there were no Child Labor laws in effect. One may notice on the list of names, two, three, or more victims with the same last name. Some young boys as young as 12 years old were killed along with their fathers in this explosion! It was necessary for them to work in order to provide for large families. There were many saddened homes on this tragic day. Mothers not only lost their husbands, but many lost young sons as well. The mine shaft itself extended straight down for over 500 feet, and then branched out into lateral, or horizontal shafts. Miners were taken down to the bottom on a primitive elevator which was operated by a cable. Only perhaps less than a dozen could be taken down or brought to the surface at one time. At the time of the explosion, there were over 200 miners in the mine. The explosion occurred at shift change in the evening, around 5 pm. Only a few severely burned miners were brought to the surface by the elevator. There were actually no survivors of this tragic explosion. There were no hospitals during this early time, and perhaps only a couple of country doctors who would visit the homes. The horribly burned miners were brought to their homes and tended to by their wives and other relatives. They watched in horror as their loved ones slowly succumbed to their injuries and burns. The vast majority of miners were never retrieved from this bottomless pit. They are entombed forever under the earth where they worked. They are entombed forever in the hearts of their loved ones, their descendants. (Below is

INTRODUCTION

depicted other names of a partial list of those victims retrieved from the Number 11 Coal Mining disaster.) Again, one can see a number of those bearing the same last name, fathers and their sons. What a tragic day in Krebs history.

THOS	BELLUTTI	JOHN	GREEN	JOEL	NICOLA
LOUIS	BLUM	CHARLES	GREGOAR	ALBERT	OLINGER
ED	BRANDON	GEORGE	GREGORI	ANTONIO	PISTOLI
FRANK	CHARLES	PETER	GREGORI	GIACOMO	PISTOTI
ANGELO	CIOCCA	DOMINIC	GRUCETTO	PAT	POWERS
FRANK	CIOLI	GEORGE	HARBOR	JAMES	QUINN
JOSEPH	CLARK	JOHN	HARLEY	JOHN	QUINN
PETER	COLLINS	FRANK	HATHAWAY	MATTHEW	QUINN
BARNEY	COMPASSO	JIM	HOPKINS	JOSEPH	ROCCO
JEAN	COMPASSO	LAWRENCE	HUNT	WILLIAM	RUSSELL
JOSEPH	CORADO	HENRY	JOHNS	LORENZO	SANTINI
ALESSO	CORANTO	THOS	KAIN	SILVER	SFERRA
JOE	CORANTO	MICHAEL	KENNEDY	LATANO	SFERRA
SANDI	DI GIACOMO	TED	KIBBLE	MICHAEL	TALETTI
MICHAEL	DI GIACOMO	GEORGE	LINDSAY	BERNARD P	TAROCHIONE
JOSEPH	EDWARDS	JOHN	LINDSAY	DOMINIC	TARRO
JOHN	FABRIZIO	BARNEY	LORENZO	ALPHONSO	THIERY
MIKE	FALLOTH	ROBERT	MCCONNELL	LOUIS	TROUBE
JAMES	FRAMER	JOHN	MCDONALD	LOUIS	TROUBE, JR
JOHN	FICCOLLETI	MICHAEL	MCSHANE	JOHN	VASSALLO
ANGELO	TIOCCO	MICHAEL	MCSHANE JR	PETER	VASSELLO
SAM A	GRENZA	JOSEPH	MILLOCHO	STEVE	VASSANO
STEPHEN	CARZINO	WILLIAM	MITCHELL	WILLIAM	WALTON
ANTHONY	GENISE	BENNETT	MOSS	JOHN	WILLIAMS
JOE	GENUSIO	PETER	MUSTATO	PATRICK	WINN

This photo shows the bottom of the Coal Miner's Monument. It is a coal miner's prayer, dedicated to the miners who lost their lives in the explosion. It was penned by a lady by the name of Margie I. Clark, and it reads thus:

COAL MINERS PRAYER

"Take a look at these hands, Lord. They're worn and rough. My face scarred with coal marks, my language is tough. But you know in this heart lies the soul of a man who toils at a living that few men can stand. There is sulfur and coal dust and sweat on my brow. To live like a rich man, I'd never know how. But if you've got a corner when my work is through, I'd be mighty proud to live neighbors with you. Each dawn as I rise Lord, I know all too well I face only one thing, a pit filled with hell to scratch out a living the best that I can. But, deep in this heart lies the soul of a man with black-covered face and hard calloused hands. We ride the dark tunnels our work to begin to labor and toil as we harvest the coal. We silently pray Lord harvest our souls just a cord near heaven when I've grown too old and my back it won't bend Lord to shovel the coal. Lift me out of the pit where the sun never shines since it gets mighty weary down here in the mine. But I'd just rather be me, Lord, though no riches I show. Though tired and weary I'm just glad to know when the great seal is broken, the pages will tell that I've already spent my time living in hell."

When I was a little boy, the road where this monument is located was called "the shaft". This, of course, was because there had been a large coal mine shaft here. Walking along this road I

INTRODUCTION 5

could still see bits of coal and black dust along the trail. Even to this day, there still remains near this monument a stone and concrete structure with bits of pipe protruding. This may have been part of a support footing for a building, or the location of an old ventilation shaft.

The area of Krebs where I grew up was called 'eleven-and-a-half, most likely because of its close proximity to the Number 11 Mine. Not far from the mine's location was a pond I fished frequently. It was called 'five pond', and was stocked with large perch, bass, and turtles!

I am a descendent of coal miners, my grandfather having worked the mines for 50 years, and my dad for a number of years, until he was almost killed in a mine in 1960. I am proud to be the son of coal miners, and I'm proud to be the descendant of Italian and Irish immigrants. Forever etched into mind is a special ritual. Every evening after a day's work in the coal mine, Dad and Grandpa would arrive at our house. They drank two cold bottles of choc beer each. Then, Grandpa would head over the hill to his house for the night. He waved goodby as he walked out the door.

"I see you onna' morn' Chass."

DEDICATION

This book Is dedicated in a special way to all of my terrific grandchildren, especially Hailee, who has expressed an intense interest from her earliest years in her ancestry. She always gleamed with delight when I related stories of my boyhood days in Krebs. We visited cemeteries where her earliest ancestors are buried. Some of the stories I shared with her were humorous; some not so much so. But, she always listened intensely, and asked questions. I hope most all of the questions are answered in this book. This book is offered also for those having an interest in the early history of Krebs, and some of the events which took place here.

I write this book also for all of my family, my brother, my sisters, and cousins, who will find in its pages, precious memories that you will recall from earlier, perhaps happier times. Stories related by our Mother and Father, by our Grandparents, and other family members will be found here. I have felt an urgency to record these events on paper for our children and grandchildren, before our generation passes, and our beautiful legacy is forgotten forever. Perhaps little did we realize in our youth what a rich tradition we have evolved from. This book, then, also is dedicated to the honor of our wonderful parents and grandparents. Perhaps the greatest gift they instilled in us was the gift of our faith. Where, or with what resources could we purchase such a gift?

CHAPTER ONE

OVER THE HILL

(Grandma and Grandpa Scarpitti, probably in their late 60's)

The blast of the loud siren stirred me from a deep sleep. I sat up in bed, rubbing the sleep from my eyes. The siren continued to echo through the early pre-dawn darkness. Then it dawned on me! It was Labor Day! The annual Krebs Labor Day Terrapin Derby! What an exciting day for an eight-year-old boy. Suddenly, my nostrils picked up the aroma of eggs frying, and Italian sausage. Oh! That's right! I spent the night at Grandma and Grandpa's. I rushed to the bathroom to wash the sleep from my eyes and comb my mop of black hair. Then I hurried to the kitchen where Grandma was already filling my plate with a delicious breakfast. I took a seat at the small kitchen table. Then she poured me a big glass of cold orange juice. She motioned with her hand, telling me in Italian to 'eat up'. I didn't need a lot of encouragement. Grandma had a special way of frying eggs which made my mouth water. It didn't take me long to finish the delicious breakfast and drink down the cold orange juice. I started to get up from the table when she jerked my arm, sitting me back down. Despite my protesting, she filled my plate again! I did manage to choke down the delicious food. Then I grabbed my ball cap and headed for the door. I couldn't wait to see my friends at the turtle races. I grabbed for the door knob, when she grabbed my arm. 'Now what?' I wondered. She opened my hand and dropped in a few coins that she retrieved from her black purse.

"Buy soda pop, canDEE." She said, in the only broken English she could muster up.

I smooched her on the cheek. "Where's Grandpa?" I queried in broken Italian.

She smiled, and managed to tell me that he was already downtown.

I hurried out the door, practically running the whole distance to the city hall. It was only 7 o'clock in the morning. I soon located Grandpa, helping to prepare hotdogs and hamburgers in the large make-shift tent in front of the city hall.

"You finally wake'a up, boy?"

"I been up a long time, Grandpa. I just finished breakfast."

"He's nothing. I eata' mine five o'clock." Grandpa said, with a wide grin. "Come'a, boy! I givea' you something."

Grandpa reached into his wallet, and handed me a crisp one dollar bill. "No spenda' too fast."

"Thanks, Grandpa." I shouted. I hugged him and headed out looking for some of my friends. Wow! With what Grandma gave me, and Grandpa's dollar bill, I probably had two dollars! That would last me all day, if I was careful. I soon located some of my pals and we headed for Johnny Lalli's drug store to buy ice cream and pop. Cokes were a nickel, and one large scoop of ice cream on a cone was also a nickel. We tried to be careful with our money, but if we should be too extravagant, there was always an old fellow by the name of Slick Ross who carried a pocket full of coins for starving kids.

These races would continue all day long, culminating with the finals around 10 pm. During those days tickets could be purchased for around a quarter, and five for a dollar. Many terrapins were needed because of the number of races. Twenty-five would compete in each preliminary race. A large circle was painted on the street between the city hall and Joe Mickella's grocery store. A barrier was created with a rope and toe sacks surrounding the circle to keep kids and dogs out. In the center of the circle stood a large steel pole with a rope attached. A large round bucket with 25 sections was placed in the center of the pole. The 25 terrapins were placed in these sections. There was a loud speaker set up in the city hall. The names of the ticket holders, the numbers on the tickets, and the addresses of the ticket holders were announced. Then the bucket was hoisted up and the race was under way. Occasionally, a turtle may wind up up-side-down and unable to compete. At this point, the race would have to start over. It is easy to see, then, that these races could take considerable time. My Uncle, Angelo Scarpitti, was frequently one of the announcers.

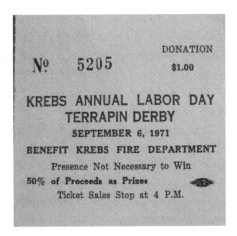

Above is a copy of a ticket sold on September 6, 1971, forty-five years ago. The price at that time was one dollar. So, in the early 50's, it would have been a fraction of that.

This grand annual event was held to help support the Krebs Volunteer Fire Department. Hundreds, if not thousands of tickets were sold, not only locally, but also throughout the country.

Many had relatives who lived out of town, or in other states, who would buy tickets. Also, 31 Highway ran right next to the city hall. So, the old timers stopped traffic coming through and invited them to buy tickets. Or, perhaps they would not let them continue unless they bought a ticket or two, especially if they had consumed a choc beer or two!

The Fire Department would start gathering terrapins at least two or three months in advance. This was a great opportunity for any kid in Krebs to make a buck. They paid ten cents for every turtle gathered. So many kids were on the hunt, that the Department would only allow a kid to sell ten turtles each. If not enough turtles were gathered, then a kid might be lucky enough to sell 20, and make two dollars! They were not hard to locate, if you didn't mind getting loaded with chiggers and ticks. I grabbed an old tow sack and headed for the woods, usually by a creek near home. I would try to get an early start because they would leave an easy track in the dew-covered grass. Many times you could walk right up on them, looking for their breakfast of bugs, worms, or grass-hoppers. I didn't take too long to gather ten or more turtles. They were usually pretty docile, especially the larger brown ones. These could reach a length of 6 or more inches. Their counterpart, the smaller black terrapins, could sometimes be more aggressive, especially if they had red spots on their front legs. They often would not retreat back into their shell when picked up, and may at times try to reach back and snap your hand.

When the Department had gathered enough terrapins, they were housed in an old jail building near the city hall. This jail would usually be filled with up-coming competitors for the race. They were well cared for, fed and watered better than they could find in the wild. They were fed watermelon rinds, and various garden vegetables, which they dearly loved. Their captivity for a time also prevented them being decapitated by angry garden growers! My dad was among this group, one who valued his garden.

The preliminary races ran throughout the day, and would not be completed until late evening. There may be as many as a hundred or more of these races. Winners would be announced, and the names posted on the side of the city hall. Following the preliminaries, there would be a short intermission as the semi-final races were prepared. Each preliminary race winner won a prize of 25 dollars. Then his or her turtle was reserved for the semi-final races. Again, competitors were announced, with the number of their turtle, and their address. There may be as many as 6 or more of these races. Winners were paid around $100. Then their turtle was reserved for the final race. There were usually around 6 turtles competing in the final race. The winner of the final race could receive up to $1000, depending on ticket sales.

The semi-final and final races were serious business! The announcer would come to the microphone. "Ladies and gentlemen, children, may I have your attention please? Please, no movement, loud talk, or running during these races. Any loud noise or movement could cause a turtle to stop in his tracks. Please, be as still as possible!"

A turtle had to completely cross the white circle to be a winner. Front legs across the line did not count. How many times I watched nervously as a turtle crossed half-way over the line, then turned back around toward the center of the ring. There were gasps in the crowd.

As a rule, the last semi-final race ran around 6 competitors. Judges were posted at various areas around the periphery of the ring. These 'judges' could be a little full of choc beer by this time. It was not unusual to see one nodding off by this time of night. Their job was to watch closely their area of the ring. When the first turtle crossed the ring, the near-by judge raised one finger. The next one crossing would receive two fingers, and the third, three fingers. These winners were then entered into the final race. Excitement filled the night, especially if one or more of the finalists should be from Krebs.

When that final race was done, I had to race for home. Mama's words echoed in my ears.

"Get right home after the races! Remember, you have to take a bath. You have school tomorrow!"

Did she have to remind me? The exciting time with the Benedictine Nuns always started on the Tuesday after Labor Day. The summer was over. It was time to get back into the books.

I was not allowed to spend nights with my Grandparents during the week, but on Fridays, or Saturdays, I was frequently heading over the hill, a change of clothes in hand. They had a nice bathroom, with a large tub. I didn't have to bathe in the kitchen in a round wash tub! My Grandparents always welcomed me with warmth and love, and plenty of good pasta to eat. Grandma was a fabulous cook, but I don't ever remember seeing

her with a cook book, or recipe in her hand. It was all in her head. She frequently rolled out her own dough, making her famous home-made noodles, which I miss still today.

The old house still stands today. Above is a photo of the south side. A primitive cellar with most of the door still present is located beneath the bedroom where I slept. Do I recall some happy and humorous times here! Many times I helped Grandpa bottle his famous choc beer in that cellar. There was one 60-watt light bulb hanging from the ceiling. It was like having candle light. Grandpa placed his brew here until fermented and ready to bottle. I was usually there to help, because it often came with a hefty award of 50 cents! He placed the quart glass bottles in a round wash tub. My job was to take a funnel, place it in the bottle, and dump a tablespoon of sugar into the bottom. Not a really hard job, except for the arrangement of the bottles, and the dim light. Some bottles received maybe two, or even more tablespoons of sugar! Grandpa took the siphoning rubber hose, and began to fill the bottles. When they were all filled, he capped them with a manual capper. Then we shook them up really well to dissolve the sugar and placed them on shelves in the cellar. The tubs were filled again and the process repeated until our job was done. Grandpa washed the crocks out and stored them in the cellar for future use. Then he turned to me and switched the light out.

"C'mon, boy. We go onna' house. Granma, he have soda pop for a' you."

I was ready for a cold drink by that time.

Spending nights there was always one of my greatest pleasures, although there was no television. Grandpa had some rules. One of them was listening to the radio until 9 pm, and then it was off to bed.

"He's 9 o'clock, boy. Time go onna' bed."

There was no arguing about staying up later. I was pretty tired from bottling choc anyway. As I retreated to the bedroom, the one over the cellar, I retrieved the silver 50 cent piece and placed it on the stand by the bed. Tomorrow I would head to Johnny Lalli's for ice cream and a Coke. I stripped down to my shorts and slipped under the covers. Grandma came in to check on me, making sure I was warm enough. Then she smooched me on the cheek, said "Good night" in Italian, and headed across the dining room to their bedroom. I closed my eyes and soon drifted off to sleep with the sound of the coal stove softly crackling as it reduced the coal to embers. Suddenly I sprang up out of bed. There was a shot gun blast! Coming directly from underneath my bed!

"Grandma!" Grandma! I shouted, making a mad dash for their bedroom. "Someone's shooting!"

Grandpa sat up in bed. "Sure, he's nothing. The choc, he blow up! Too mucha' sugar onna' the bottle! Go back onna' bed!"

I retreated back to the bedroom, burying my head under the covers. The next couple of blasts were not quite so terrifying. I soon drifted off back to sleep, sleeping soundly until early the next morning. It was Sunday, and Grandpa was up early. The first morning Mass at St. Joseph's was 6:30 am, and we would be there. Grandpa entered my room about 5:30. It was still dark outside. The rooster was crowing his alarm.

"Sure, get up! Grandma, he fix'a the breakfast for a'you. Then we meet Shoe Peg for a' the Mass."

I quickly got dressed in my Sunday clothes, and headed for the kitchen table for Grandma's terrific breakfast. Then Grandpa and I walked out onto the porch and down to the street light on the corner. Here we waited for Shoe Peg to give us a ride to church. Shoe Peg was my Aunt Mary Ann's Dad, and he and grandpa were neighbors and close friends. He derived his name from his occupation, a shoe cobbler. He owned and operated a small shoe repair shop on South Main Street in McAlester. It's a trade practically forgotten today. When shoes wear out, people merely discard them and buy new ones. During those early days, shoes could be re-soled, or have new heels put on for a nominal cost. I recall Shoe-peg re-soling shoes for me for a cost of 50 cents or a dollar!

We waited patiently under the street light. Grandpa took out a match and lit up a cigarette, one of his favorites, Chesterfield. Maybe because my Dad's name was Chester. Anyway, I thought so as a small boy. Soon we heard a garage door screech open.

"Yep! Sure here comma' Shoe Peg." Grandpa said, blowing smoke from his cigarette.

A black car rolled up. It was a 1948 Ford, four-door. The windshield and the back window had a bar in the center, dividing them in two. I took a seat in the back, while Grandpa sat up front with Shoe peg. They chatted merrily on the way to Mass, but when we entered the church, there was absolute silence. We were in the presence of God, in the Blessed Sacrament. He was present in the tabernacle. There was reverence and awe.

After the Mass, Shoe-peg brought us to Grandpa's house. He was always invited inside for coffee. It was a ritual. If it was cold winter time, the coffee may be spiked with a little whiskey to heat things up. After the visit and coffee, Shoe Peg would head home. Grandpa always attended the early Mass. There were always chores to do, even if it was Sunday. Early the next morning, work began all over again in the coal mine. I hurriedly changed into my old clothes. This was another opportunity to earn a buck from Grandpa. We may pull weeds from his garden, or burn brush along the trail leading up the hill to our house. He

was never idle. When noon was approaching, Grandma would appear on the porch, beckoning us to lunch. This was usually some of her special spaghetti with sauce and meat balls. If only she had had the time to have a restaurant. She would have outdone all of the restaurants today! Above is shown the old shanty. A sidewalk made of stones is still visible leading to the shanty. This is a special place in my memory. A place where hogs were butchered and processed, sausage hung up, and cracklings made and dried for eating. I can still hear the sounds. Seems like everyone in the neighborhood was there to help out with this event. Tables were set up outside to process the pork. To the right of this shanty, in the past, there was a large black kettle. It has been confiscated by one of the other grandchildren. This large kettle served multi-functional uses. One of them, of course, was to process the butchered hog. To my recollection, everything was placed into this kettle, except the head! Of course, the hog was beheaded and gutted. Hind quarters, front quarters, shoulders, all were placed into this iron kettle to be cooked. This large iron kettle was designed with an open pit underneath for building a fire. The kettle was filled with water, and when boiling, the butchered pork was placed inside for cooking. Not much was wasted. I recall from my early childhood a delicacy of pickled pigs' feet and ears! They were never one of my favorite foods as a child. I had tasted the pickled feet. They were almost edible! Ice cream and candy always tasted better. One of my favorite things from these seasonal hog butcherings were the delicious cracklings which my Grandpa fashioned. These were similar to bagged pork rinds available in stores today, only better. These were made from the fatty outside layer of the pig's skin. They were boiled in the kettle, like the other pork. Grandpa had a type of old press with a heavy lid. It resembled a pressure cooker. These cracklings were taken from the boiling pot and placed in this press. A crank pressed and squeezed toward the bottom of the press, removing as much grease as possible. Then they were wrapped and placed on a shelf in the shanty for drying. Depending on the size of the hog, there may be as many as three or four of these round crackling cakes. After they seasoned for a few days, I would be robbing those shelves.

During these early days, these heavy black kettles served a variety of purposes. There were no washing machines, so clothes, including nasty coal miner's clothing, were washed in these kettles. They were then rinsed, wrung out by hand, and hanged on a clothes line. The famous choc beer, too, was cooked in these kettles. This choc beer derived its name from the Choctaw Indians who were the first to brew it. The recipe was later adopted by the early immigrants who dubbed it "choc beer".

One Saturday morning I raced down the hill. Grandpa was going to be brewing his choc. I always liked to watch, and maybe even help. Before I reached the house, my little ears picked up the sound of cursing and swearing in both languages! I approached the cellar door when Grandpa came flying out, carrying one of the 20 gallon crocks.

"Dirty some-un-a-bitch!"

My eyes were probably the size of half-dollars. "What's the matter, Grandpa?"

"Damn mama cat! He havea' babEE onna' crock!"

He proceeded to reach down into the furry crock, retrieving baby kittens. Then he slammed them down on the stone patio, squishing them under his feet!

Grandma appeared on the front porch, screaming in protest, but it did not deter him. I don't know how long it took for Grandma to speak to him again. She was a cat-lover. There were a number hanging around the house all the time. There was a large opening, a crawl space, on the south side near the porch. Cats would frequently retreat under the house for safety. I bet the mama cat was under here at this time, watching in horror as her babies were annihilated. Luckily, there were no animal rights people around in those early days. No one desecrated Grandpa's crocks! That was sacred ground. He did manage to scrub the crocks out, and the brewing process was underway, after he had me to dispose of the kittens in an abandoned well, of all places!

The abandoned well was located across the street from where my car is parked in the above photo. It has been filled in today, thank God! The cedar tree was present when I was a little boy, and it is still in good shape today. There was a side walk of stone, and a rock bench located under the tree. Grandpa would frequently be seated there in the summer, in the shade, enjoying his glass of cold choc beer. He would frequently scold me in the hot summer time when I came down the hill to visit.

"Hey, boy! Put the hat! You gon' get the sun stroke!"

Above is a picture of the old house from the north side. In earlier days, there was a large porch on the right side, and another porch behind on the left side, facing east. Some years after Grandma passed away in 1983, Uncle Angelo moved into the home and reduced it in size by removing a couple of rooms and some porches. My brother, Sonny, did the carpentry work. Today the old house stands vacant with a good acre and a half of land, land my grandfather farmed by hand. Today all that remains is the memories of a coal miner's grandson.

CHAPTER 2

GRANDPA JOHN

In the photo above, Grandpa John Scarpitti is standing near the porch on the south side of the home. The rock patio mentioned earlier is clearly visible. Grandpa frequently dressed this way, winter or summer. He preferred long-sleeve white shirts, and gray kahki pants. He usually had a straw hat on his head, especially in hot summer time.

Grandpa John was born in 1890, and came to this country when he was 16 years old. Evidently there were not many opportunities for employment in his home country. He first settled for a short time in Steubenville, Ohio, working in the steel mill. He soon came to Oklahoma and settled in Krebs to work the coal mines here.

Grandpa and Grandma came from Castiglione, Italy, which was located in the central to southern part of the country. They knew each other as children in their neighborhood.

Grandpa John came to America in 1906. When he came to Krebs, he lived with the Sellars family, who were cousins. He made his home with this family until 1910, when he married Grandma Concetta. Seems everyone in Krebs had nick-names during these early days. Grandpa was referred to as "Juan-a-la-Cioli", which translated to "John of the Sellars clan".

Grandpa John and Grandma Concetta were married on April 10, 1910, at St. Joseph's Catholic Church in Krebs. Their 'delightful' honeymoon took place in what was referred to as "the big shanty". This building was located on the property where our family lived. The property and old house were given to us by Gandpa Scarpitti, who later moved his family down the hill to the old Massaro home. Grandpa Scarpitti did not earn a great deal of money as a coal miner, but he was careful with what he did have, and was able to put some money away, even with raising a large family. He did not own a car and never learned to drive one. There was no health insurance, house insurance, or social security benefits in those days. One could barely make ends meet as it was, yet Grandpa evidently did have a life insurance policy on himself, and he was able to buy property in the area at a nominal cost. He did own several lots in the area.

GRANDPA JOHN

When I was a little boy, he disclosed his saving plan to me.

"Boy, you makea' the dollar, put fifty cents onna' bank!"

I later came to realize that Grandpa, even with a large family, was putting back half of what he earned! I've tried to adopt that plan today, but I can only manage, at times, to put back one-tenth of my meager earnings.

Grandpa moved his family over the hill to the Massaro home in 1936. He purchased the home for the whopping sum of $400! That also included about one-and-a-half acres of land! It is believed that he probably cashed in a life insurance policy to purchase the home.

One cold winter morning in 1937, about a year after Grandpa moved his family into the 'new' home, Grandma got up to begin the morning, fixing breakfast for her family. Grandpa rolled out of bed and threw more coal in the stove in the dining room. Then he took a seat and looked out the window near the porch. He savored a delicious cup of hot coffee before breakfast and another day in the coal mine. Suddenly his eyes caught a frightening sight, smoke drifting off of the house. He dashed out onto the porch, spilling coffee on himself. He hurried back into the house.

"Get out the bed! Hurry up! The house, he burn!"

Uncle Orland, 18 at the time, dashed to the porch on the east side, clad in long-handle underwear and bare feet. He scaled the column on the porch, and with bare hands, ripped the burning wood shingles from the roof and tossed them to the ground. The house was saved through the heroic efforts of Uncle Orland.

Grandpa John was fortunate to never have been employed in the Number 11 mine. He originally worked in the No. 5 mine in Krebs, and later worked in a mine in Haileyville, east of Krebs. Here he was in part ownership with six or eight other men, my dad among them. He was also fortunate to never have received any severe injuries in his 50 years of shoveling coal. My mom recalled as a young girl that the only accident she remembered was when a coal car ran over his big toe, crushing it! He had to remain at home for a day or two. Luckily, he was never in a mine explosion, but he witnessed one or two, and was involved in recovery efforts. Funeral homes were scarce in those early days. Families were often responsible for preparing bodies of loved ones for burial. Grandpa related to me his share in this.

"I been shave plenty dead man, boy."

In other words, he was frequently called on to help prepare these bodies for burial. This was, of course, before my time. However, as a child, I recall a tradition of bodies being brought to their homes. They would lie in state, with their families keeping vigil over them until their funeral.

When Grandpa John moved his family down the hill to their new home, Mom and Aunt Rose, her older sister, were already married. At this point, the girls were gone. Grandma Concetta stopped making her famous home-made bread at this point, because she did not have the extra hands. This bread making was quite a process, and will be described in a later chapter.

GRANDPA JOHN

I am the youngest of four children, but I am fortunate enough to have witnessed Grandpa John's long life in the coal mine. When I was about a fifth grader at St. Joseph's Catholic School in Krebs, we had an associate pastor, Father John Scheller. Father Scheller had expressed an interest in visiting the mine in Haileyville where Dad and Grandpa worked. He wanted to experience for himself the hardship of working in the mines. After checking with Dad about this, it was arranged that Father and I could visit the mine one afternoon. So, one afternoon, after school, Father Scheller and I drove to the mine in Haileyville. I recall a long steep slope leading down into the shaft of the mine. Coal cars were attached to a strong cable which lowered them down into the mine, and hoisted them back up again when filled. The cable was operated by electrical power. Father Scheller and I were equipped with helmets and seated in the back of an empty coal car, facing the opening of the mine. A signal sounded. The car began its slow descent into the steep mine. A miner was riding with us, his carbide lamp providing dim light in the coal car. As it grew darker, I watched as Father Scheller crossed himself with the sign of the cross. I watched in horror as the rectangle of light at the entrance of the mine grew smaller, smaller, finally disappearing all together. It was pitch black, except for the dim light of the miner's lamp. It seemed an eternity before the car reached the bottom of the mine. Several lateral shafts extended out horizontally and were supported by strong timbers. The sounds of picking, shoveling, and machinery filled the darkness. The sound of "swooshing" startled me. Suddenly Grandpa was in front of the coal car. He had slid down a shoot from a shaft above. His carbide lamp illuminated his black dusty face.

"Hey, boy! You come, watcha' me work?"

"Grandpa! Is that you? You scared me!"

"Sure, he's me! No be 'fraid. I black from work!"

Dad soon emerged, as black as Grandpa. He looked at Father Scheller.

"Hi, Father. Think you'd like to do this for a living?"

"I think not." Responded Father. "I'd best remain a priest."

We bid good-by to Dad and Grandpa, and after being shown a few other areas of the mine, we began our ascent to the surface. I was never so happy to see the little rectangle of light appear once again. When we reached the surface, Father Scheller crossed himself once again, and I imitated him, happy to be back in daylight again. The Italian coal miners were often called "Dagos". I learned the meaning behind this later in life. When they left for the mine it was dark. In the mine, it was dark. When they returned home it was dark. So, when they emerged from the mine, they would wonder: "Where'd the day go?"

That one visit in the coal mine was enough for me. I would find a different job when I grew up. I would, however, in the summer time ride to the mine with Dad and Grandpa. There was a creek near the mine, Brushy Creek, which was good fishing. Dad would frequently let me ride along and fish in the creek while he and Grandpa worked. There was always an admonition.

"Watch out for the Copperheads. I don't want to haul you to the doctor for a snake bite."

GRANDPA JOHN

"OK, Dad. I'll be careful".

So, while Dad and Gramps worked in the mine, I fished. I don't recall ever bringing any fish bacK home with me. They would be pretty rank at the end of the day.

During the early to mid-fifties, Dad drove a blue 1948 Buick. This was a long heavy car, which to me, resembled an up-side-down boat. The car needed shocks. Riding to the Haileyville mine on the two-lane Highway 270 was like taking a roller coaster. On their way to the mine, another rider was always included, Dan Rich. He was a distant cousin of Grandpa John. Dan was a rather small man, and he always sat in the back next to me, while Grandpa sat in the front. There were no seat belts in these early times. We picked up Dan and headed for the mine. Dan always sat straight up on the seat, resting his arms on the back of Grandpa's seat. Grandpa turned around, and the two would be chatting all the way to the mine, some broken English, some Italian. Dan's head bounced off the head-liner, as the old Buick rocked up and down on the rough highway.

Occasionally there would be another fisherman along to accompany me, John DeLana. John was about three years older than me, and was an avid fisherman. Sometimes we would be dropped off at Dow Lake, located near the highway, and three or four miles west of the mine. Dad felt a little more secure, as I had an older boy with me. Mom always packed us some lunch to carry us through the day. Here we remained all day long, until Dad picked us up along the highway on the way home. If fish were not biting in the Lake, Brushy Creek was nearby, and we would try there.

One day while fishing at Dow Lake with John DeLana, I began to feel sick and feverish. It was hot summer time. For whatever reason, while waiting for Dad, I decided to lay on a flat rock directly in the sunshine, instead of picking a place in the shade. When Dad pulled up and took a look at me, he was ready to clobber me. He felt my forehead.

"Boy, you're burning up with fever! Why the hell were you laying in the sun? You should have been in the shade. Your mom's going to have a fit!"

I didn't have a ready answer. I just lay down on the back seat on the way home.

The picture to the right captures a scene where Grandpa John is almost smiling, very uncommon. The photo was taken in 1957. It shows him with his arm around grand-daughter, Lucille Massaro, daughter of Uncle Bill and Aunt Rose. They were visiting from Akron, Ohio, an annual summertime vacation. Lucille was frequently clad like this in order to get an Oklahoma tan. Grandma Concetta did not like her attire, and frequently protested, telling her in Italian to put some clothes on!

The area of Krebs where we and our Grandparents lived was known as "eleven-and-a-half". The reason for this was that the

GRANDPA JOHN

number 11 mine had a secondary shaft located in this area. Miners who lived in this area could enter at this secondary shaft, and not have to walk to the main entrance some distance to the south. As a little boy, exploring this area to the north of my Grandparents' home, there was still a large sink hole in a field, which I'm sure now was the remnant of this secondary shaft. Any animal unfortunate enough to fall in here was doomed, unless he had wings!

When Grandpa John worked in the No. 5 Mine in Krebs, he walked to and from work. Frequently he had to stop by Joe Mickella's grocery store on the way home to buy groceries. Then he loaded a couple of sacks with groceries, hefted his miners bucket in one arm, and headed for home, probably a mile away. He was frequently exhausted from the day in the coal mine. There was an irritating neighbor who lived in the area who was constantly stopping Grandpa to complain. Here's the rest of the story.

Grandpa and Grandma had a son, Herman (Cap), who was severely retarded. His mind was probably that of an 8 to 10- year old boy. He was at this time in his early thirties. Cap loved to roam around the neighborhood, the town. He never really bothered anyone, or disturbed the peace. He dearly loved animals, all kinds…..cats, dogs, horses, cows. He never did any harm to any of them. He just loved being around them.

This irritating neighbor, Mr. Sid Johnson, was constantly stopping Grandpa on his way home, complaining about Cap. He was bothering a dog, or a cow of his. So, you guessed it. He caught Grandpa on the wrong day. Grandpa was walking by his house on his way home, when the door screeched open. Mr. Johnson appeared on his porch. He descended the steps and walked to his gate near the road. Grandpa knew what was coming.

"Mr. Scarpitti, your boy, Cap, he........."

He didn't get to finish the sentence. Grandpa set his miners bucket, and the bags of groceries on the ground. Then he reached over the gate, grabbing Mr. Johnson by the collar.

"Sure, Mr. Johnson, I tire as hell. You stoppa' me every day, tella' me some bull shit 'bout my boy, Cap. Sure as hell, he never do you nothing. Sure, you stoppa' me one more time, Mr. Johnson, I gon' beat the hell out you."

He let go of Mr. Johnson's collar, and he slowly slumped to the ground wide-eyed. Grandpa picked up the grocery bags, his miners bucket, and started off for home. Mr. Johnson never stopped him again!

After some years of working in the coal mine, Grandpa Scarpitti thought he had had enough. He would move the family back to Ohio and again try employment in the steel mills. Uncle Angelo, the baby in the family, was three years old at the time. My mom was probably ten or twelve. I recall her speaking of this time, which was very trying for Grandma Concetta. Uncle Cap may have been eight or nine years old. Akron Ohio was much different than living in the small community of Krebs. Uncle Cap liked to wander around. There was a great deal of traffic. Grandma Concetta worried herself sick that he would be run over and killed. Grandpa finally realized the stress she was under. He called mom and Aunt Rose aside after a short stay in Ohio.

"Sure, you mama, he get sick. He worry 'bout a Cap. Fraid he get kill onna' street. Sure, we go back onna' home, Krebs."

The family was soon packed up and boarded the train back to McAlester, where they were picked up at the depot by Shoe Peg, the only one with a car in the neighborhood. After this, Grandpa John returned to work in the coal mine. He never left Krebs again.

Grandpa loved his choc beer and his cigarettes. He always had a few cold bottles on hand for visitors. Visitors were invited to sit at the table, or on the porch if the weather was nice. He would retreat to the fridge and retrieve a quart bottle of cold choc. Glasses would be brought out and then he would pop the cap on the bottle. Blue smoke would usually drift up from the bottle.

"Ah! Them's good one!" He would smile.

He was right. The colder it was, the better it tasted. Even as a young boy, I knew this. He had a small glass reserved for me.

He could not stand to be out of cigarettes. When his supply ran short, he would put a couple of dollars in my hand.

"Boy. Go onna' Joe Mickell'. Buy me some smoke."

"What kind do you want, Grandpa?

"Bringa' Lucky Strike. He no haveum', bring Chestfield."

GRANDPA JOHN

(Grandpa John on right, Uncle Bill Massaro in middle, Uncle Dominic Di'Frangia on left) Uncle Dominic was Grandma Concetta's brother. The similarity is striking.

During these early days, it was not uncommon for a young boy to buy cigarettes for his dad or grandpa. There were no laws preventing this. Grandpa would give me a couple of dollars.

"Get the smoke! Get you canDEE, or pop."

I always hurried back to Grandpa's house where he would immediately open a pack of cigarettes and puff away while I snacked on my candy. It was not unusual for him to smoke a couple of packs a day. No wonder this along with black lung did him in at the age of 72. After a couple of cigarettes, he would usually head for his massive garden to do some work. I was permitted to go in, so long as I didn't stomp on any of his plants.

He would allow me to pull weeds or maybe hoe around some of his plants. One day the curiosity of a young boy hit me. Grandpa's garden was neat, but the rows of plants were very crooked.

"Grandpa. Why are Daddy's rows so straight, and yours are really crooked?"

He looked at me, rather disgustedly. "Sure as hell, he never make no difference!"

I never questioned him about this again. Later I surmised, well maybe he could get more plants in a crooked row!

On Sunday afternoons, Grandpa John and his friend Shoe-peg, had a ritual. After lunch, they would usually head to the old Knights of Columbus Lodge near down-town Krebs. Here they spent most of the afternoon, visiting with old friends, playing cards, morra, or bocce, and drinking beer. I was often with them. Again, Grandpa supplied a dollar for candy or pop. The bar tender was a short little Italian man by the name of Dominic Ross. He looked at me through thick glasses. Then he questioned me.

"Hey, boy! What you want? Soda pop? What kind? Dr. Pep? Pepsi Col? Double Col?"

Double Cola was a soda pop brewed right in Krebs by the Silva Family. It was pretty tasty. I scratched my head under my ball cap.

"Well, give me a Double Cola and a Hershey Bar." I handed him the dollar bill.

He popped the cap off the cold bottle of cola, handed me the candy and change. He smiled at me.

"No drink and eata' too fast! You getta' sick."

I assured him that I would go slow. Then I headed outdoors where there were three bocce courts set up. It was fun to watch these old-timers play this game similar to bowling, only with smaller balls. The dimensions of the courts were measured out and sectioned off with rail road ties. The dimensions may have been roughly 20 feet wide by 100 feet or more in length. There were two opposing team members at each end of the court. A small white game ball was tossed out into the middle of the court. It was about the size of a golf ball. Each team member had two balls each. The game began by a team member rolling a ball toward the game ball to get as close as possible. Then the opposing team member rolled a ball to see if he could get closer to the game ball. The opposing member then took his turn. When one side was finished, the opposing members at the other end of the court took their turns. The balls were colored, perhaps green for one team, and blue for the other. The team with the ball, or balls closest to the game ball took the round. The game was scored like horseshoes. The first team to reach 21 points won the game. Some of these players were quite skilled. They could toss their ball, knocking their opponent's ball away from the game ball and getting the point.

One old gentleman who I really enjoyed watching was Mario Fenoglio. Instead of rolling his ball like a bowling ball, he studied the situation closely. He judged distance well. Then he tossed his ball high into the air. Amazingly, most of the time his ball landed very near the game ball. It was amazing to watch him.

As the afternoon wore on and the old timers consumed more beer, they became more competitive and loud, but always in a fun way. There were never any fist fights.

Grandpa John was not big into these games. Sometimes he would play card games, but never bocce or morra. He just enjoyed his time visiting with his mining buddies.

The other game played was one called "morra". This game was played with the hands. The court was a large rectangular table. There were four team members on each side of the table. This was a numbers game. The numbers were called out in Italian, from one to ten. The game was played like this. Opposing members faced one another across the table. Simultaneously, they would call out a number at the same time throwing down on the table a number of fingers with one hand. For example, if one member called out the number 7, throwing out 4 fingers, and his opponent throwing out 3 fingers, then he won the round, provided his opposing member did not call out the same number. If so, it was a tie, and they would play again. If a member won the round on one side of the table, he would challenge the next opposing member on the other side. The game, again, like horseshoes, was won when a team reached the number 21. This game was also fun to watch, and the team members could become quite loud, as they tossed out fingers with one hand, and held a beer in the other! The losing team usually had to buy a round of beers for the winners.

Pictured above is the site of where the old out house was located at my Grandparents' home. It is filled in now. The old outhouse was located over an abandoned well, of all things! At least one did not have to worry about emptying it out from time to time. In the background is visible a portion of the green field which was a segment of Grandpa's garden. Also, visible to the right in the background is the site of another well. This one has not been filled in, but is covered. There are perhaps two other wells on the property. This was necessary in earlier times when city water had not yet been installed. Imagine the hardship of those times, when water had to be carried to the house in buckets for drinking, cooking, or bathing, not to mention that water had to be hauled from the well to fill the old iron kettle for washing clothes!

As a little boy, I had two friends who lived in Grandpa's neighborhood, Billy Jeff Miller and Ronnie Weehunt. Several times I would stray over the hill to my Grandparents' home for a visit. Grandpa would relate to me that my friends were looking for me.

"Beely JEFFur, he look you". Or perhaps, "Ronnie WeeHUNT, he look you."

I failed to appreciate in those early days how Grandpa had to learn to communicate with others, no matter how broken his English was. He had to somehow communicate with his fellow workers in the mine, who mostly spoke English, except for his Italian buddies.

In addition to my Uncle Cap, who as mentioned earlier, was severely retarded, there was also another big man in the area by the name of Franky Pupius, who was also retarded. He perhaps had somewhat more mentality than Cap. He, too, would wander around Krebs and the surrounding area, even walking to McAlester, about three miles to the west. He wore big ankle-high boots, and had a gigantic stride. It was stated that one time a neighbor spotted Franky walking along the highway toward McAlester. It was hot summer time. He thought about being neighborly. He stopped his car near Franky.

"Hey, Frankie! You want a ride? Hop in!"

Franky bent down, peering into the window.

"No! Franky walk. Franky in hurry today."

That story always brought a lot of chuckles from the citizens of Krebs.

At times, Franky would wander down into my Grandpa's neighborhood. Grandpa John was always friendly to him, offering him something to eat or drink. One day I approached Grandpa's porch on one of my many visits. He was sitting on the porch with his glass of choc in hand. He looked at me.

"Sure, Frang Poop' he was over in here. Sure, he say this, anna' that, anna' them. Sure as hell, never say nothing!"

Of course, this was Grandpa's way of saying that Franky rambled on and on, without saying anything that made any sense.

Franky was a big, strong man who did not take teasing or joking lightly. Some policemen in McAlester found this out the hard way one afternoon. They were accustomed to seeing him walk along the streets, or the highway leading back into Krebs. One day they thought they'd have a little fun with Franky. Three or four of them stopped near him in their patrol cars, as he was leaving McAlester on his way to Krebs. They exited their patrol cars and approached Franky. One of them blurted out.

"Hey, Franky! You been walking around our streets too much. We're going to have to arrest you and put you in jail for a while."

They reached for Franky's arm. He jerked his arm from them.

"Franky no go to jail!"

In a blur, the officers found themselves tossed onto the roof of their patrol car. Franky began his long stride to Krebs. To my knowledge, Franky was never approached by the policemen again.

There were few old Italian men of Grandpa's time who had cars, and knew how to drive. I'm not even sure they had a driver's license. Most of them drove their old cars in first or second gear everywhere they went. The cars ranged from 48 to 51 or 52 Chevys or Fords. You could pick up the sound for blocks away. One of the old gentlemen, Frank Testa, would frequently visit Grandpa for a cold glass of choc. He drove a light blue 1950 ford. Grandpa would pick up the sight and sound from a couple of blocks away.

"Yep. Sure here come Frang' Test'."

He retreated into the kitchen, retrieving a cold bottle of choc beer. He brought my little glass to me. We sat on the porch, sipping our choc and talking. Then Frank would fire up the old car, and we could pick up the sound as he made his way back home, several blocks away. The old timers would ride the clutch, too, which made the sound even more deafening, not to mention the damage to the clutch! Dominic Ross, mentioned above, was also notorious for driving this way. He also owned an old, probably 1950 Ford. He would frequently peel out, throwing gravel out behind him. Popping the clutch, we called it.

I especially recall one hot summer night I spent with my Grandparents. Again, I was sleeping in the bedroom located over the cellar. There were no air conditioners. Grandpa and

Grandma had the only box fan in their bedroom. I opened the windows as high as possible to try and catch some breeze. As it began to cool a bit, I dozed off. Suddenly I heard the sound of footsteps. I opened my eyes and sat up in the bed. Was it a ghost? I rubbed my eyes. It was dressed in white! Oh, it's only Grandpa. But, what is he doing? Is he walking in his sleep? He unlatched the screen door and went outside. I was scared. I sprang from the bed and raced into Grandma's room. I grabbed her arm, shaking it. Then I tried to relate to her in the best Italian I could muster that Grandpa was walking in his sleep. Reluctantly, she rose from the bed as I led her to the porch near my bedroom. There we found Grandpa sprawled out on the porch, clad in his white long-handle underwear.

"Grandpa!" I shouted. "Are you ok? I thought you were walking in your sleep! I was afraid you were going to fall off the porch."

"Sure as hell, I no walk onna' sleep. He's too hot onna' bed. I come onna' porch, cool off. Go back sleep!"

Here I was too hot, sleeping in my shorts, and Grandpa was sleeping in woolen long-handles? That didn't make sense. Then I realized, maybe the sweat and the breeze from the porch had a cooling effect.

During these early years, too, Grandpa John was quite involved with other activities. He was a member of the St. Joseph's Our Lady of Mount Carmel Men's Club, as well as a member of the Knights of Columbus. During the Fourth of July celebration, he was often in charge of helping to operate a fireworks stand located along Highway 31 on the west end of Krebs. Of course, other old timers were also involved, Frank Testa, Dominic Ross, Shoe Peg, and perhaps others. There was always some choc beer iced down behind the tent when they became thirsty. After several bottles of choc, they could become a bit tipsy. Little boys, of course, are always curious. One little boy approached the stand. Grandpa came up to wait on him. He continued to pick items up, examining them closely, and quizzing Grandpa.

"What does this do? What does that do?"

Grandpa turned to him with a look of disgust.

"Sure, I never know what the hell he do! Put the match on 'em!"

The little boy dropped the items, darting away from the stand as quickly as possible. Grandpa retreated to the back of the stand for another cold choc.

Grandpa was also in charge of purchasing and storing fireworks for the annual Mount Carmel Celebration on the 16th of July. This grand celebration was originated in Italy and incorporated into St. Joseph's Parish at the turn of the century. Mom related that when she was a little girl, this celebration lasted a couple of days. It was always celebrated on the 16th, no matter what day that may fall on. When it was incorporated at St. Joseph's, it always fell on the Sunday immediately following the 16th. Here we had an all-day celebration, including games for children, the Italian games of morra and bocce, music, and a grand luncheon, followed by a fire works display in the evening.

In earlier times, Mass was celebrated in the evening of the 16th. At the consecration of the Mass, two men were signaled to set off a deafening blast of dynamite in the ball park. This signaled the beginning of the celebration.

Mom related that there was always a large Ferris wheel set up, and various bands would play music throughout the night. At the conclusion of the ceremony, there was always a large fire-works display in the form of an American flag. She also related to me that at one of these celebrations the weather turned ugly. There was a violent storm, with wind, rain, and hail, not to mention the lightening. People ran for protection. Many retreated to local homes, where they were welcomed inside. Grandpa had wall-to-wall people in his house until the storm passed by. They were total strangers! Grandma protested. But, Grandpa told her there was no other place for them to go. They had to help them. This was part of Grandpa's heart, his generosity. It extended not only to his neighbors, but total strangers.

Grandpa stored volumes of fireworks in the old shanty pictured earlier. Grandma worried constantly that the kids would get into the fireworks and be hurt. But Grandpa reassured her that they would not bother them. I'm sure they were threatened with their lives.

During these early times, just about every family in the Krebs area heated their homes with coal. In the yard of every house there was a nearby coal pile. Grandma and Grandpa Scarpitti had one in their yard on the north side of the old home. I would often bring in coal for them in the winter time. There was a coal bucket which probably held about five gallons of coal chunks. The bucket was metal with a wide spout at the end for pouring in the coal. The bucket would usually be filled in the evening and placed near the stove for night time use. The large round iron stoves were located in the central part of the house, usually in the dining room. Bedroom doors were left open at night so that, hopefully, the heat would radiate into the cold bedrooms. Heavy quilts were still required on really cold nights.

Grandpa Scarpitti's generosity to his neighbors was an inspiration to me, even as a little boy. There was a black gentleman who lived in his neighborhood by the name of John Chapman. John was very poor, living in a tiny one-room shack to the northwest of my grandparents' home. Grandpa John would watch for his passing by in the cold winter time. When he caught sight of him, he would step out onto the porch.

"Hey, John Chap'! Takea' some coal for a' you stove"!

Mr. Chapman always carried with him a tow sack over his shoulder. Here he would place scraps of iron or glass pop bottles, or anything else which he might sell for a few pennies. He would always thank Grandpa John, as he placed some chunks of coal in his bag to keep himself warm during the night. Then he would head over the hill to his one-room shack.

Grandpa John loved mushrooms that grew in the wild, and he would frequently take a tow sack and head for the nearest creek to find his treasures. The best time to find them was in late fall or early winter. It was a cool time of the year. Mushrooms growing on timber or old logs were good to eat. He would never pick mushrooms from the ground. They could be poisonous!

One cold early winter day Dad and Grandpa took Dad's old Buick and went to Peaceable Creek south of Bache to search for mushrooms. They had a pretty good day of it, but Grandpa had a mishap. A nice crop of mushrooms was growing on a large log which was leaning over the creek. He crawled out onto the log to retrieve his treasures. There was a loud "CRACK". You guessed it. The log gave way. Grandpa tumbled into the creek, sack and all. I'm not even sure if he retrieved the mushrooms. Dad hurried him back to the old Buick, turned the heater on high, and headed for home. When I learned of Grandpa's demise, I rushed over the hill to his house. He was seated near the old coal stove, wrapped in a blanket, a cup of hot coffee in his hand.

"Grandpa! What happened to you?"

"I falla' onna' creek! Sure as hell, he's col'!" He shivered.

I did, however, see a sack of wet mushrooms near the kitchen table!

On another excursion involving Dad and Grandpa John, Dad was hunting rabbits near Peaceable Creek. Grandpa was along, hunting his mushrooms again. Grandpa did not own a gun, or hunt. For some reason, Dad had no hunting license. Along came a game warden! Dad was soon faced with a hefty fine. Dad was a little ticked off as the two made their way back home. Without thinking how it sounded, Grandpa spoke up.

"Dirty bashth! Sure, we oughta' been bump em' off, throw em' onna' creek!"

GRANDPA JOHN

I'm not sure if Dad had a response to this, but I do know there were some choc beers consumed when they got home.

Grandpa John was a hard-working man, supporting a wife and six kids on a coal miner's pay. When he arrived home from the mine, however, his work was not yet finished. There were hogs and chickens to be fed, not to mention the large garden to be tended. Mom related something to me that has remained in my mind all these years. After supper Grandpa John would head for the garden. Here he would plant, cultivate with a primitive hoe, weed, whatever needed to be done in his large garden. Nothing was wasted, including the space. Vegetables from here were canned in glass mason jars and stored on shelves in the cellar. If he ran out of daylight, he hung a lamp in one of the pear trees located in the garden. When he could go no more, he retreated to the house, cleaned up and went to bed. His day started before daylight. He must have wondered. "where'd the day go?"

Grandpa John spent 50 years working in the coal mine. He retired in 1957. Shortly after that he became ill with clinical depression, something he had suffered with most of his life. In those early times, it was not clearly defined, and there were no medications to treat it. Grandpa could not adjust to retired life. He felt his life was over, that there was no meaning in his life any longer. He would lay on the couch, holding his chest, moaning in pain. Some could have been imaginary; some was undoubtedly suffering from the years of breathing coal dust, black lung. He considered doing himself in. He felt he was a burden to Grandma, and his mom, Great Grandma Grace, who was living with them at the time. One late night there was a frantic knock

GRANDPA JOHN

on the door. Dad rose from the bed. Grandma was standing with tear-filled eyes at the door. Mom rose from the bed when she heard Grandma's voice. In Italian, she related to mom that Grandpa had wandered off into the garden, near a well, and was threatening to throw himself in. Dad and Mom rushed over the hill with her, and finally convinced Grandpa to go back into the house, that he was scaring the two Grandmas nearly to death themselves. Shortly after this incident, Grandpa John was admitted to a mental hospital in Vinita, Oklahoma. The only treatment available for his condition at this time were shock treatments. After a series of these, he returned home a couple of times for short visits, but would have to return soon to the hospital for more treatments. On his return to the hospital, he would always have an admonition.

"Sure, he's last time! I never come home again."

In the Spring of 1962 his prediction became true. I was a senior in High School at the time. We received a call that Grandpa John had taken a turn for the worse. He had developed pneumonia and was slipping into a semi-conscious state. Uncle Angelo and I made the trip up to Vinita. We took my godfather, Pug Rich's 1956 Ford. I was only 17 and had just recently received my driver's license. Uncle Angelo allowed me to drive some of the way up. He was giving instructions on how to drive safely. When we arrived at Grandpa John's bedside, he was unconscious. He did not respond when we talked to him. It was a sad sight for me, as a young man, who had spent so many happy times with him. His nurse approached and related to us how Grandpa had been talking to her about what he knew best, coal mining. Shortly after this, he slipped into a coma. Uncle Angelo and I kept a vigil throughout the night, remaining near his bedside. We knew his time was short. When I could stand it no longer, I would retreat to a nearby lobby, and recline on a sofa. Around 4 in the morning, Uncle Angelo came sobbing into the lobby where I was half asleep.

"Bill, come in son. Grandpa, he's gone! Oh, what are we going to tell Grandma?" He sobbed uncontrollably.

We retreated to his bedside and knelt down. We said some prayers. I grabbed Grandpa's rough, calloused coal miner's hand. It had grown stiff by this time.

"Oh, Grandpa! I'll never forget your hands!" I sobbed.

After the funeral home picked up Grandpa to return him to McAlester, Uncle Angelo and I went to a small motel to try and rest for a couple of hours before we made the trip back home. Neither of us could sleep. Uncle Angelo sobbed in his nearby bed, and I could not forget Grandpa's hands. Finally, we got dressed and went to a café for coffee and some breakfast. A juke box was playing a song, "Little Jimmy Brown". To this day, when I hear this song, it takes me back to that time.

As we approached my Grandparents' home on our arrival, Uncle Angelo sobbed once again.

"Oh, Bill! What are we going to tell Grandma?"

Grandma met us on the porch, and with tear-filled eyes said in Italian, "Come in, Angelo! Please come in!"

We both hugged her and cried. Then I retreated back up the hill where I fell into the arms of Mom, and sister Marilyn.

"Grandpa's gone, Mom. Grandpa's gone." I cried.

They both hugged me tightly, and my mind raced back to my visit in the coal mine, and Grandpa's blackened face.

Above is pictured the tiny kitchen where Grandma fixed her delicious sausage and eggs for me in the morning. The small table on the right was used for preparing the eggs and sausage for frying. I have never tasted eggs as delicious as what Grandma cooked. This was one of her favorite items. She often ate eggs two or three times a day. The cholesterol did her in at age 93!

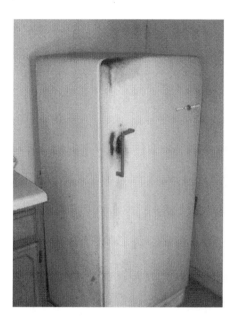

(This tiny refrigerator still remains in the house today, in the small kitchen at the other end. Grandma Scarpitti was very short, so household items could not stand very tall, or she could not reach them. This included a telephone which was installed in the home in later years. It hung on the wall, about four feet from the floor.)

(Above is shown part of the old chimney at the top where the stove pipe was inserted. This is located in the central part of the house in the dining room. At the bottom is a small cabinet where various items were stored. I recall shoe polish, rags and cloths, and even various medicines. I recall one of my overnight stays when I became nauseous. Grandma retrieved some Bromo Seltzer from here. I was soon comfortable again.)

GRANDPA JOHN

(Above is the wedding picture of the happily-wed couple! I suppose smiling was not cool in 1910. Grandpa John was 20 years old here, and Grandma Concetta was 22. His hair was long, but Grandma's was much longer, as seen above. On one of my visits to their home when I was a little boy, I made a remark about Grandma's long hair. Grandpa smiled at me.)

"He's nothing! You should seen him onna' ol' country. He's hair, he been touch the ground!"

CHAPTER 3

GRANDMA CONCETTA

Above Grandma Concetta Scarpitti is standing by Aunt Mary, Uncle Orland's wife. This photo was taken in June, 1956. I was 12 years old. They are standing near St. Joseph's Catholic Church in Krebs. The stained- glass window is visible in the background. Aunt Mary was short, but Grandma Concetta was shorter, standing only a little over four feet tall! Here she would have

GRANDMA CONCETTA

been 68 years old. As seen, her hair was silver, but her eye brows remained black. When my little girls came along later in life, they were frightened by her appearance. But they soon learned that Grandma Concetta was gentle in nature.

When Grandma Concetta first arrived in Krebs, she lived with her sister Mary Massaro. She was married to Rocco Massaro, who was not related to Uncle Bill. When Rocco died, Mary moved to Ohio and married Grandpa John's brother, Joe.

Above, Grandma Concetta is pictured on the left, and her sister, Mary on the right. Neither lady was very tall, but again, Grandma Concetta was the shorter. Again, notice the similarity! They are standing in front of my Grandparents' home. The window in the background is where their bedroom was located.

The porch on the left faced the west side. I spent a lot of time as a little boy, playing on this porch.

Life was not easy during these early times. I mentioned earlier how hard Grandpa had to work. Life for Grandma Concetta was not much easier. Her day would begin each morning by rising early from the bed. Breakfast had to be prepared early before Grandpa headed off for the mine. Some children were in school, so they had to have breakfast, and a lunch prepared for the school day. To make matters worse, if it happened to be a day when bread was baked, Grandma had to rise much earlier than her usual time. She would have to incorporate the help of either Aunt Rose, or Mom. They were young school children by this time. An argument would ensue. Mom related how Aunt Rose was notorious for not wanting to rise from the bed. She would argue.

"I did it last time! It's your turn."

No matter how much my mom protested, Aunt Rose always seemed to prevail. It always seemed to be Mom's turn. She would have to rise from the bed and help Grandma Concetta prepare dough for the bread. The flour and water were prepared in large pans. The dough was kneaded until it was ready to place in the pans. At this point, Mom could return to bed for a time before breakfast.

After Grandpa had left for work in the coal mine, and the children were off to school, Grandma Concetta's work was just beginning. An old outdoor bake oven was located adjacent to the big iron kettle. This oven was equipped with a space underneath for a fire. Grandma would place wood here and begin the fire. The outdoor oven was fashioned of brick or rock, quite large with a roof on top. There was a door to seal the contents inside. When she thought that the oven was warming up, she would bring the pans outside. She baked six or eight large loaves at a time. Hopefully this would be enough to feed a hungry coal miner and six children for a day or two. Ironically, there were no handy thermometers then to gauge the temperature of the oven inside. How did Grandma know when the oven was heated at just the right temperature to place the loaves inside? As a little boy, I questioned Mom about this one day. What she related to me was fascinating. Grandma would open the oven door and place her hand inside. Then she began to pray the Lord's Prayer, in Italian, of course. If she could pray the entire prayer without having to withdraw her hand, the oven was just right. If she had to remove her hand, the oven was too hot, and would burn the bread. She waited for a time and tried again. What an oven thermometer!

As a child growing up here, most old home places were equipped with such outdoor ovens. I know of none remaining today. Outdoor pets, especially dogs, would retreat under these ovens when spring storms approached. On the hill where I grew up, we had an old gray dog named "Snippy", who always retreated under our bake oven when a storm approached. He always turned around with his head facing the opening. Here he remained until the storm passed by. The ashes did not seem to bother him in the least.

Grandma Concetta not only baked her famous bread here, but also, washed clothes in the adjacent black kettle. This was a difficult task again. Water had to be hauled from the nearby well, a fire started, and the water heated up. Then the process began. The laundry included dirty coal miner's clothing, and all the children's clothes, not to mention bed linens and towels. The process would have taken most of the day. There were no washing machines or clothes dryers. The items had to be wrung out by hand and hung on a clothes line for drying. Then she would rush into the house to start supper. After supper, again, there were no automatic dish washers. Hopefully to clean up the kitchen and wash the pans and dishes, she would get the help of mom and Aunt Rose. Then it was off to an early bed, for the process would begin all over the next morning.

During these early times, there were no televisions. Most families had one radio in the house where they could listen to music and various programs, and the news. I recall gathering around the radio at my grandparents' home with them, and even at our old home on the hill. People would socialize more during these early times, because there was no television or computers to occupy their time. Consequently, they would gather at one another's homes from time to time for a visit. So many times, my grandparents' rock patio outside would be filled with visitors, enjoying a pleasant evening, drinking choc beer, wine, laughing and enjoying being together. My mom shared a fascinating story from her childhood.

There was a custom of gathering at one home or another on Friday nights, after a hard week in the coal mine. One Friday night, it was Grandpa's turn. He had the cold choc and wine ready, bread, and Italian cheese. Then, the men began to show up. Seats were filled around the round dining room table. Grandpa got the deck of cards and the fun began. The old timers were smoking cigars, cigarettes, and pipes, and swearing in both languages. As the night wore on they became louder and louder as they consumed more choc beer. The house was filling with smoke. Some of mom's siblings were quite small at the time. Grandma Concetta was doing her utmost to get the children to sleep, but it was impossible with a house full of smoke, and the shouts of the drunk men. It was approaching mid night. Grandma could take it no longer. She tossed the quilts aside and rose from the bed. She emerged in the dining room in her night gown, brandishing a broom. She shouted and waved the broom in the air to the astonishment of the drunken guests. Then she let them have a dose of her mind, in Italian, of course.

She waved the broom in their faces. "You men, go home now! You fill the house with smoke, you scream and curse, keeping my kids awake! Get out of here!"

The men grabbed their coats, and without a 'good-by', darted out the door. Then Grandma Concetta turned her attention to Grandpa John.

"I carry the water and make the choc beer for you. It takes me a lot of time, and you drink it all up in one night with your buddies. I'm not going to make the choc for you again."

Without hesitating, Grandpa turned toward her.

"You make em' alright."

GRANDMA CONCETTA 60

That was the end of the story. The next morning Grandma headed for the well with her bucket. The brewing began again.

I don't believe that I would have the nerve of my Grandfather. I know what my wife would say.

"If you want a six pack the Circle K is right down the road."

(I'm not sure where the above picture was taken, but it shows some "happy" campers around the dinner table. From right to left, Aunt Rose, Great Grandma Grace, Grandma Concetta, Aunt Mary, and Christine.)

GRANDMA CONCETTA

Grandma and Grandpa later upgraded their home, having modern conveniences that we lacked up on our hill. They installed a bathroom, fully furnished with tub, stool, and sink. Grandma Concetta, however, felt it was not proper to use the bathroom in the house. So, winter, summer, rain or shine, she would retreat to the outdoor toilet. Even in the dark of night time. It took some years before she became comfortable enough to use the bathroom in the house, wash her hands in the sink, and return to her chores.

Sometimes when I visited, she would send me to the chicken yard to retrieve any eggs that the hens may have left behind. There were several small compartments in the hen house for the hens to do their thing. Peculiarly, most of these compartments contained a ceramic door knob. The belief was that when the hen rested on this knob, it would prompt her to deliver an egg or two. It must have worked. These compartments were usually where I found the large brown eggs. I would take them to Grandma, and she placed them in the fridge. The eggs were fresh and nutritious, the yolks almost appearing red in color.

Grandma Concetta derived her name in a peculiar way. She was born on December 8, the feast of the Immaculate Conception in the Catholic Church. The name "Concetta" is believed to be derived from this feast day, from the word "Conception". Because of this, her birthday was always easy for us to remember.

Grandma Concetta was usually of a cheerful nature. Many times, when I approached her house as a small boy, I could hear singing coming from inside. There were two or three old hymns that she would frequently sing in her native tongue. Even when she would leave her house and walk along the path leading up the hill to our home, she could be heard singing these hymns.

When I visited, she always had a special treat for me, one that I can still savor today. It was her special homemade bread and butter. By this time, the outdoor oven was no longer in use, but she did a great job with the gas oven. I would be provided with a couple of large slices of this and a glass of soda. As I savored this, Grandma Concetta would recline in her arm chair in the living room and read her large-print Italian prayer book.

One of my fondest memories of Grandma Concetta was when she attended Mass on Sunday mornings at St. Joseph's. She always attended the 9am Mass. After the Mass, she would gather outside the door with a small group of her Italian lady friends. Here they would chatter in their native tongue for at least 30 minutes, sometimes more. They were catching up on the latest news in the area, or perhaps gossiping? They put me in mind of a little huddle of clucking hens! After this session was over, Grandma and I would make the trek back to her house, where she would always have a delicious Sunday dinner prepared soon.

One of the things I was envious of in these early days concerned the Sacrament of Confession or Reconciliation as it is called today. Practically all of these Italian women, and a few men, could only speak in their native tongue. In all likelihood, the priest hearing their confessions could not speak their native tongue, and yet they received absolution for their sins. As a small

GRANDMA CONCETTA

boy, this did not seem fair to me. It seemed to me that they were getting a free pass! But, such is the mercy of God.

I often think of what courage and faith it must have taken for Grandma Concetta to leave her parents and siblings behind and come to America as a young woman. My mom often spoke of this, recalling how Grandma would often cry, realizing that she would never see her parents and some of her siblings again. It was something that had to take great courage, faith, and love for a man named "John".

I was only 17 years old when Grandpa John left this world, but I will forever hold an image of Grandma Concetta in my mind. We were in the family car making our way to the cemetery to lay him to his final rest. Grandma was rocking back and forth, crying, and sobbing. In her native tongue, she moaned.

"My John, my John! Where have you gone now? My John, my John!"

Everyone in the car was crying with her. She could not imagine her life without her John.

Ironically, to my best recollection, he was laid to rest on their 50th wedding anniversary, their golden, making it even more difficult.

After his passing, the family felt like Grandma Concetta would not last long. We were wrong. She lived 20 more years, passing in 1982. During those years, Grandma passed her time praying her prayer book, and watching Lawrence Welk on television. My mom made the trip over the hill every day for a visit, and to fix her hair. After Grandpa passed, Mom and Dad moved in with her for a time to keep her company and to look after her. While they were in Grandma's home, the old house on the hill caught fire one hot August day, and burned to the ground. After this, Dad built a new home on the same site, and Mom and Dad moved back up on the hill in the late 1960's. Mom still checked on Grandma Concetta every day, and took care of all her needs.

I would go down the hill from time to time to mow her grass with a push mower. A humorous incident occurred one time. A friend, Larry Finamore, came down to Grandma's to help me with the mowing. We thought we were doing a fine job, until we approached the living room area. The mowers were pretty loud. The living room screen door popped open. Four-feet-tall Grandma Concetta appeared frantically waving her arms. It caught our attention. She shouted to us in Italian.

"Go the other way! I can't hear the television."

Lawrence Welk happened to be on at that time.

Grandma Concetta faired pretty well until she was almost 93. At this point she began to have a series of mini-strokes. One of her favorite candies were M&M's, no peanuts. She preferred the plain ones. She would retrieve a few from her bag in the refrigerator now and then. When I would ask her for some, she would count out two or three. The same way with her pennies which she kept in a black purse behind a large wooden trunk in her bedroom. When I asked for some, she would count out ten for me, not a penny more! When she began to have the mini-strokes, she would ask for her candy. We would retrieve some for her and place them in her mouth. She chewed but could not swallow. The delicious chocolate would have to be spit out. Shortly before she ended up in the hospital, I visited her at her home. She was lying in her feather bed, Mom and Uncle Angelo nearby. She grabbed my hand, looked into my face, and made a request in her Italian tongue.

"Pray for me, because I'm going to die!"

I related to her in the best Italian I could muster up that she was not going to die yet. She had more years left.

She managed to give me a weak smile, shaking her head "no", her eyes filling with tears. At this point I left the room, for I didn't want her to see me crying.

Shortly after this she ended up in the hospital. She lingered for a week or two, always asking for her "canDEE", which we placed in her mouth for her to chew on. Her swallowing became increasingly worse, and the candy had to be spit out. By the grace of God, she did not suffer long. After a few days more she suffered a massive stroke which took her life. She passed in 1982, almost 21 years after her beloved John (Giovanni) left this world. The two are buried in Mount Calvary Cemetery in McALester. Buried next to them is Grandpa John's father, Stephano Scarpitti, and their son, Herman (Cap), who will be described in a subsequent chapter. With Grandma Concetta's passing, a generation of the Scarpitti family had gone to their rest. I will always treasure their memory, and the valuable lessons they both taught me concerning life and what really matters……family.

CHAPTER 4

GREAT GRANDMA GRACE

(Great Grandma Grace standing in front of my Grandparents' home on the south side near their bedroom. This picture would have been taken in the mid 1950's.)

Great Grandma Grace was Grandpa John's mother. She came from New York to live with my Grandparents in the mid to late 1950's. Her husband, Great Grandfather Stephano, mentioned above, died in 1935. Mom mentioned how he was infected with what was then called "yellow jaundice", which was probably a form of hepatitis, or something worse. Great Grandma Grace would place him outside in the direct sun light, which was then believed to help affect a cure. Of Course, it proved fruitless, and after some weeks he succumbed to his illness.

As you can see in the photo above, Great Grandma Grace was chunky. She was strong and high-spirited. Her hair was white and her eyes were blue. She had no teeth in her mouth, but could eat anything she wanted, including the hard-crusted Italian bread. She would sometimes tease me by grabbing my forearm and munching on it. It hurt! Those gums were like teeth!

Like Grandma Concetta, she could speak little English. She did learn to call us by name as best she could. I was "BailEE". My brother was "SonEE". My sisters were "Phoolis ANN", and "Moolan JANE". Dad was "Chass", and mom "MarEE". Their accent, even in the broken English, seemed to be on the last syllable.

Even though she was in her nineties, Great Grandma was meticulously clean. In the hot summer time she was known to bathe as much as three times a day. In her cooking, she was also immaculately neat and clean. Pots and pans had to be scrubbed inside and out. All table utensils, although clean, were washed again. While we kids were in school, she would often show up at our house on the hill. Here she prepared a delicacy for us, after everything was scrubbed of course. She created a wonderful treat, making her own dough and incorporating mashed potatoes inside. Today these are called "Gnocchi".

Great Grandma's. however, were called "cavatilli", and they were much more tender and juicy. To top it all off, she **created her**

own home made sauce which was the greatest I had ever tasted. I could not wait to get home from school. My nostrils would pick up the pleasant aroma from blocks away! There was always enough to feed the whole neighborhood. Pans were dished out to the Pulchnys' next door, to other neighbors, and some were transported down the hill for Grandma and Grandpa. Then the cleanup process began. It was an all-day affair. While she and mom were preparing this delicacy, Great Grandma Grace would relate stories of her childhood in Italy. One has stuck in my mind over the years. As a young girl, her family owned a herd of sheep. She would have to go tend to these sheep every day, seeing that they were fed, watered, and protected. One day when she went, she too became thirsty. There was a clear stream nearby. She went down to take a drink of cool water. As she drank, a huge snake came swimming by. She related how she almost fell into a spell, a trance. This soon passed and she resumed her task. After supper that evening, she became quite ill and retreated to her bedroom. During the night, she became increasingly more ill. There was little opportunity for a doctor visit in those days. Her parents tended to her the best they could. She was afraid to close her eyes, for she feared she might die. She did recover, and after a few days she was back to tending sheep. Perhaps the large snake expelled some venom into the water, but the tough Italian girl had it over on the snake!'

I'm not sure how much education Great Grandma had, but she surely could read to a degree at least. In her room at my Grandparents' home, she had a large wooden trunk which contained a number of large books resembling encyclopedias, in Italian of course.

(A view of the bedroom where Great Grandma Grace slept, the window facing north)

When Great Grandma arrived here, Grandpa John had already upgraded to a degree, installing an open space gas heater in her room. On cold winter days, she would sit on her bed, doing one of her favorite things, knitting. She had baskets of yarn which she put to good use. She created sweaters, mittens, even stocking caps, and distributed them freely. If I should go down on a cold winter day, with snow on the ground, she would catch me before I went outdoors. She equipped me with mittens and a stocking cap. Then she would point to the outdoors. She would always appear on the porch after 30 minutes or so, and beckon me back inside. She always removed the wet mittens and stocking cap, placing them near the coal stove to dry. If my hands were frozen, she would retreat to the small kitchen and retrieve a pan of warm water. In here she would place my hands until they were thawed. After my hands returned to normal, and the mittens and stoking cap were dry, I was permitted to go back outdoors for a time to play in the snow. Soon Great Grandma would appear on the porch and beckon me back inside.

Without doubt, Great Grandma Grace was a hard-working woman. In addition to all her cooking, she also helped out in Grandpa John's huge garden. Not only that, but she also created her own sizeable garden near the chicken coup. She dug up the area with a shovel or spade, and planted tomatoes, peppers, and other vegetables, including her favorite, cantaloupes. These she called "mushk-ma-LONE". When I went over the hill for a visit, we would frequently share one of these delicacies. They were always cold, sweet, and delicious.

She not only tended her own garden, but also cared for the gardens of a couple of other old Italian women in the neighborhood who were unable. She would arrive on their porch, carrying a spade, and the work would begin. She cultivated, planted, even watered the gardens of her old friends. When harvest time arrived, she picked the vegetables and delivered them to her friends.

Great Grandma Grace and her daughter-in-law Concetta respected one another, but they kept their distance. Perhaps Great Grandma Grace felt like Concetta was not quite good enough for her son, John. A little late at this point! Or, perhaps

GREAT GRANDMA GRACE

Grandma Concetta thought that Grandpa was paying too much attention to his mom, and neglecting her. Who knows? Nonetheless, you could pick up on the division. Lunch times were divided. Grandma Concetta ate hers first on the small kitchen table. Great Grandma Grace kept a wary eye out, and when Grandma Concetta was finished and no longer in sight, she would prepare her lunch at the kitchen table. Many times, this consisted of white spaghetti covered with red wine. This was always accompanied with some Italian bread. Perhaps this is why she attained the ripe old age of 101. I never developed a taste for it.

Great Grandma Grace had another peculiarity. For whatever reason, she began to hide certain food items from Grandma Concetta. Perhaps she wanted her own stash. Eggs from the hen house, bread, bananas, apples, and various other food items were placed in one of the drawers in her chest in the bedroom. At one of mom's visits, she detected a rotten odor. After investigating, she discovered the rotting items. I don't believe she got a decent explanation from Great Grandma. At any rate, the ruse did not stop.

During these early times, it seemed that all the old Italian women wore knee-high woolen hose, winter and summer. Great Grandma was no exception. One day my mom went over the hill for a visit. She noticed a blood stain on one of Great Grandma Grace's hose. She related to her in Italian that it was nothing to worry about. Despite her protests, Mom pulled the hose down and almost fainted. Before her eyes was a cut extending from just below the knee almost to the ankle.

"Grandma! What happened?" Mom asked in Italian.

It seems Great Grandma was making a trek to the outhouse a few nights before. She stepped from the porch near her bedroom, and somehow her foot caught a rake in the yard. This mishap created a large gash on her leg. She told mom that she tried doctoring it with various medicines she had. However, mom could tell that the wound was infected. Despite the protests of Great Grandma, she was transported to the doctor, given some shots and antibiotics, and the wound was healed after some time.

Great Grandma Grace was hard-working, but also fun-loving. She enjoyed visits at our house, where she dearly loved her time with Dad. She did not savor choc beer, but Dad always had some of her favorite wine available. She would have a drink or two with him, and would even dance around the kitchen with him. Dad also developed a special bond to her.

She was a devout Catholic, praying the rosary daily, and never missing Sunday Mass. She traveled from my Grandparents' home to the church on foot, about a half-mile away. The road she traveled is now Blake Avenue. During these early times, it was called "the rough road", and rightfully so. There was no gravel. After a heavy rain the road would become hazardous. Deep ruts were created, and passing was very slippery and treacherous. Passing cars would often slide off into the ditch and have to be pulled out. Nonetheless, this was the route Great Grandma traveled on her journey to the church. Rides were never accepted. Rain or shine, hot or cold, ice or snow, Great Grandma walked. She considered this as part of her sacrifice to attend Mass. Along the way, she prayed her rosary, and in the spring time, she picked wild flowers growing along the road. Little did I realize then what an example she was setting for me, what an inspiration she was to me as a little boy. Only later in life do we realize that "more faith is caught than taught". Perhaps it was through her inspiration, her example, her legacy, her faith, and that of other family members, that our Lord opened my eyes, and called me forth to serve him as a Deacon.

When Grandpa John became ill with clinical depression, his mom, Great Grandma Grace could hardly take it. He would lie on the sofa, moaning. At the sight, she would retreat, crying, to her bedroom. She could not stand to see her son suffering like this. Finally, in about 1960 or 61, she could stand it no longer. She packed her trunks and returned to her native Italy. There our Lord called her in her sleep at the age of 101.

CHAPTER 5

UNCLE CAP

(Above, Uncle Cap stands near the west side of the home. Old houses are visible in the background. The cedar tree he is standing near still remains today. The hedge has been removed. Probably from the 1940's)

Uncle Cap was born after Mom, probably around 1918. He was the first of the boys. He was born severely retarded, possessing the mind of probably an 8 to ten-year old. His real name was Herman. The name "Cap" derived from his habit of usually wearing a ball cap. He frequently dressed as shown above, or in overalls. As with all persons who are mentally challenged, he could be quite temperamental at times, exhibiting swift mood swings.

Uncle Cap loved to follow the old road graders around Krebs as they tried to smooth the roads and make them somewhat passable. I recall accompanying him on some of these ventures. Anything that caught his eye was picked up and stored in his overall pockets. This might include pennies, marbles, bobby pins, even bits of shiny or colorful glass. When he arrived home from his trek, these items were sorted and stored in drawers in the large dining room china hutch. These were his treasures, and they were not to be touched without his permission.

Mom recalled from her childhood something interesting and amusing. She and Aunt Rose would rise early in the morning and begin to fix their hair for another school day. Perhaps they would need an extra bobby pin or two. They would approach Uncle Cap.

"Cap, we don't have enough bobby pins to fix our hair. Can we borrow some of yours?"

If he was in a good mood upon arising from bed, they might hear this.

"Sure! Take as many as you want!"

On the other hand, if he had arisen in a foul mood, the response might be quite the opposite.

"Hell no! Not one! Not even for a dollar!"

No matter how much they pleaded with him, he would not be persuaded to change his mind. So, Mom and Aunt Rose had to attend school with their hair half-done!

Sometimes Grandpa would give him a dollar or so to go to Joe Mickella's store for candy or pop. His favorite soda was grape, or strawberry. As a little boy, I would wait for Uncle Cap to pass by our house on his way back from Joe Mickella's. Maybe he would share his candy with me. Again, his mood dictated this.

"Sure! Take all you want! I won't even charge a dime!"

If, on the other hand, he preferred to be selfish on this day, he might respond in a different way.

"Get out of here! Hell no! Not one piece! Not even for a damn dollar!"

He would wrap his hand around the top of the paper bag and stomp out the door toward home.

During these early times, Mom was 'fortunate' enough to have an old wringer type washing machine in the shanty over the cellar. This was quite a chore, washing clothes for herself, four children, and dirty coal-miner's attire. Water had to be carried from an outdoor faucet to the machine. Uncle Cap would often visit when she was preparing to wash. She could only hope that Uncle Cap might be in a good mood.

"Good morning, Cap. It's wash day. Will you carry some buckets of water for me?"

She might catch him on a cheerful day.

"Sure! Where's the bucket? I'll carry every bucket for a quarter."

If she caught him on a sour day, she was in trouble.

"Hell no! I'm not carrying one damn bucket! Not even for a dollar!"

One thing that always intrigued me about Uncle Cap was that despite his mental capacity he was quite fluent in English and Italian. I suppose he grew up this way, finding it necessary to speak English to his siblings, and Italian to his parents. I recall one night that I spent there. Uncle Cap and I slept in the same room, the one over the cellar. Grandma, as usual, had breakfast prepared when we arose from our beds. I headed straight for the little kitchen table. Uncle Cap soon followed. For some reason, he did not want the delicious eggs and sausage that Grandma had prepared. He protested in Italian.

"I don't want this stuff, Ma! I don't want this stuff!"

I knew enough Italian to pick up what he was saying. Grandma had spoiled her baby "Herman'. She soon had before him what he requested.

Grandma and Grandpa, and other old-timers in the area had a special name for him, something that sounded like "ManDOOCH". This was a term of endearment. Its meaning was something like "little Herman". This was how he was referred to throughout his neighborhood of eleven-and-a-half. All of the old-timers in the area knew him, and knew of his mental condition. They looked upon him as a little boy, and welcomed him into

UNCLE CAP

their homes. If he should be visiting one of them when the church bell at St. Joseph's rang for the noon Angelus, it was time for him to return home for lunch. They would remind him of this.

"ManDOOCH". The church bell rang. It's time for you to go home now for lunch. Your mama will worry about you."

He would usually comply without hesitation.

Uncle Cap would often wander around the town of Krebs, visiting with people, and buying candy and soda pop with money Grandpa provided him. During these days, many people sold choc beer to supplement their meager earnings. This helped them survive from check to check. Some customers were known to consume a little too many of these choc beers. One day Uncle Cap was making his way back toward home when two men stopped to offer him a ride. They did not know him, nor did he know them. He accepted the ride. When the men began to question him as to where he lived, they realized that he was mentally challenged. In the car, Uncle Cap could not give them directions. The men became frightened, and for whatever reason they took him out of town a short distance east of Krebs to an area known as Richville. Here they dropped him off, hoping that he would find his way back home. Uncle Cap was lost. It was approaching winter time and night fall. He was clad only in his overalls, no jacket. Uncle Cap soon found something he loved, cows huddled in a barn. He soon joined them, keeping them company and petting them. The farmer had fed and watered his cows, and had returned to his house for the night.

UNCLE CAP

Here Uncle Cap spent the night, huddled near the cows for warmth. In the early morning, the farmer returned to check on his cows. As he approached the barn he heard the sound of someone sobbing. He soon discovered Uncle Cap huddled near the cows.

"Hey, boy! What's your name? What are you doing here?"

Uncle Cap was too cold and scared to respond.

The farmer soon realized that he was mentally not right. He led him to his house and gave him hot coffee and some breakfast. Uncle Cap was still too afraid to respond to any questioning. This man was a stranger.

Finally, the man managed to coax him into his truck and take him to the Krebs area to see if anyone knew him. Along the way, the farmer again attempted to derive a name.

Weakly, Uncle Cap responded. "Scarpitti".

'Scarpitti'. The man scratched his head. Where had he heard that name before? On entering the city of Krebs, he began to enquire about a Scarpitti family. Where did they live? He soon received the answer he was looking for, and Uncle Cap was delivered home safe and sound. I'm sure it was a sleepless night for the family, inquiring everywhere throughout the night where Cap might be. It was a great relief to see him step onto the porch that morning. I'm sure Grandma had him a nice breakfast waiting.

UNCLE CAP

(In the photo below, Uncle Cap stands in the middle, Uncle Orland on the right, and Uncle Angelo on the left. Behind them is a jewel, approximately a 1936 Ford Coupe)

Uncle Cap was lost more than one time. He would sometimes forget the hour, that it was growing late. He was held spellbound by his love and attachment, especially to cows or horses. There was an old man in the neighborhood by the name of John Homer. Mr. Homer knew Cap well, as he would frequently observe him petting his horses and cows through the fence. One evening late, Cap was with his cows, but Mr. Homer was not aware of it. He placed his cows in the barn for the night, but did not realize that Cap was among them. As it began to grow dark, he closed and locked the door to his barn. Cap remained in the dark, again huddling near the cows. Supper time came and Cap was nowhere

UNCLE CAP

in sight. Grandpa knew that the search soon would be on. He took his lantern and headed outdoors, inquiring of the neighbors whether they had seen Cap. At first, there was little response. No one had seen the lost Cap. Then Grandpa happened to think. One neighbor he had not asked yet was Mr. Homer. He lived nearby. Grandpa knocked on the door of his one-room little house. The door screeched open.

"Hey, Mr. Scarpitti! Anything wrong?"

"Sure Cap, he never comea' home. You been seen um?"

"I havn't seen him. He hasn't been around here today. I just put the cows away for the night."

"Sure, we bet' look, Mr. Home. Cap, he mighta' be onna' cow."

"Sure, Mr. Scarpitti. Give me a minute."

The two soon retreated to the barn where Mr. Homer unlocked the door. Grandpa lifted the lantern for light.

"Cap. You, over inna' here?"

Cap soon emerged from behind one of the cows. Sheepishly, he approached Grandpa John.

"Whatsa' matter you? I tella' you, comma' home before he get dark. Eata' supper."

Mr. Homer felt awful. "I'm sorry, Mr. Scarpitti. I should have looked more closely before I put the cows away for the night."

"He's ok, Mr. home. He's no you fault. Cap, he should never been round over in here."

Again, Cap made it home safe and sound.

Grandpa John realized Cap's mental status, but thought, mistakenly, that he could discipline him through certain methods. I recall one of these attempts quite vividly. Uncle Cap would repeat things he had heard, even certain curse words. I approached Grandpa's porch one day, when I found the two standing there, a dispute going on. Grandpa was standing in front of Cap, holding a hot pepper up to his face.

"Say em' gin', boy! I put the hot pepper."

"Son-of-a-bitch." Cap responded.

Grandpa swiped the hot pepper across his tongue.

"Say em' gin'."

"Son-of-a-bitch".

"What the hell?" Grandpa swiped the pepper across his tongue again.

"You gon' say em' gin', boy? Say em' gin'."

"Son-of-a-bitch."

Before this session was over, Uncle Cap's tongue was blistered and Grandpa was out of hot peppers. He did not realize that Uncle Cap thought he was obeying him!

UNCLE CAP

Uncle Cap loved music on the radio, especially listening to Bob Wills. He would sometimes carry a small harmonica in the pocket of his overalls. He would take it out and blow on it from time to time.

When he approached his forties, Grandma and Grandpa were growing too old to care for him. The constant vigilance that was necessary to keep up with him was too much. He could at times become enraged with anger for no apparent reason. This happened one cold winter morning after Grandpa had left for work in the mine, and Grandma was left alone with him in the house. He arose from bed in a foul mood. Grandma could not calm him down. He began to curse and kick the coal stove until it was nearly turning over. Grandma was screaming for him to stop. The sound caught the ears of a neighbor man who happened to be passing by. He somehow managed to get Uncle Cap calmed down and made sure the coal stove was secure before he left. Following this incident, Grandma and Grandpa were convinced that they could no longer handle the burden. Uncle Cap was committed to the mental institution in Vinita, Oklahoma, where he remained for the rest of his years. We went to visit him as often as possible. His request was always for a grape soda, which he delighted in. He would wander around the grounds, picking up sticks and tossing them to the side. This, too, was one of his peculiarities.

Uncle Cap lived a pretty long life, considering his handicap. He was almost 52 years of age when he passed from this life in 1969. Little Herman, 'ManDOOCH', went to join his papa, Grandpa John in heaven.

UNCLE BILL AND AUNT ROSE

(Uncle Bill Massaro, probably in his early 50's)

    Uncle Bill was a very comical person, and I always felt he could have made a living as a professional comedian. He was also very talented at playing the accordion and the harmonica. This is where I developed my love for the harmonica. I could listen to him play on my Grandparents' porch for hours. It seemed that the more choc beer he consumed, the better he played. He always brought from Ohio a large chromatic harmonica which had a button on one end. This button could be pushed in and out to produce the sharps and flats. He was very skilled, making the harmonica sound like several instruments playing at the same time. He played a variety of old waltzes and polkas. Two of his

UNCLE BILL AND AUNT ROSE

favorites and mine were "The Tennessee Waltz" and "The Beer Barrel Polka". He would have everyone dancing around on that porch. He could also play a number of old Gospel hymns. I recall a time or two when he took his harmonica to St. Joseph's parish hall where the men's club were meeting. He would entertain them for hours with only his harmonica. He would even take requests from those wanting to hear certain songs.

In his earlier years, he often played baseball with my dad. Uncle Bill would often play centerfield, for he was fast on his feet. Thus, the nickname "rabbit". Dad would often be the pitcher, where most of his talents were. He, too, would sometimes play in the outfield. They were both skilled baseball players, and I often felt that were there more scouts around in their day, they may have been major leaguers.

Uncle Bill would frequently have the little kids laughing. He could imitate the sounds of certain birds. He would chirp and whistle while reaching into his shirt pocket. Little kids would think there was a bird inside. Finally, he would make a fluttering sound while looking up, indicating that the bird had left his pocket.

Uncle Bill only had a grade school education, but he was employed in a machine shop in Akron, Ohio. Here he remained for a number of years, finally retiring after many years of employment. He was a skilled machinist.

He and Aunt Rose would drive down to Oklahoma every summer to spend a week or so at my Grandparents' home. One summer they came down, and Uncle Bill was driving a blue-and-white 1958 Chevrolet which he had recently bought new. I recall him talking about having engine trouble with the car shortly after he bought it. He took it bacK to the dealer a couple of times, but the problem was not fixed. Finally, he had had enough. He took it back to the dealer a final time. The shop foreman approached him.

"Mr. Massaro! You back? We'll try again to fix the problem."

"You're not going to fix nothing! You're going to put a new engine in that car!"

"But, Mr. Massaro, I can't do that!"

"You're not talking to a woman here, sir. You're going to put a new engine in that car."

Uncle Bill soon had them convinced. He got his way.

He often acted out in pantomime stories of some of the Sellers bunch, who had little formal education. Some could not read or write. He depicted how a couple of them pretended to read to convince others. One scene he pantomimed out was of two of them sitting opposite one another reading newspapers. They were up-side-down!

Another scene involved one of them who owned an old model t car, but never really learned to drive it, at least very well. He depicted a scene where the fellow was driving the car along a trail in a field when he got bogged down. He was wearing elbow-length white driver's gloves. He got out of the car, walking around it, shaking his head, and waving his hands in the air. It probably did little good to extract the car.

(At left, an oldie but goodie. From left, Aunt Rose Massaro, Tony Massaro (I'm sure kin to Uncle Bill), and my mom in her teen years)

Another comical scene Uncle Bill described involving the Sellers bunch was quite comical. One of the old fellows had a couple of sons. None had received much education, and were quite simple-minded. Their papa was constantly being pestered by a neighbor who was always there trying to borrow something. So, sure enough, one day the pesky neighbor arrived in the yard. One of the sons was outside playing. The old neighbor approached him.

"Hey, is your dad home? I need to borrow a rake."

"Just a minute. I think he's in the cellar."

The boy hurried down into the cellar. "Hey, dad! Our neighbor's here. He wants to borrow a rake."

"Oh, hell, son. Go tell him I'm not home."

The boy rushed out the cellar door. "Hey, mister! My dad told me to tell you he ain't home!"

So much for simple-mindedness.

UNCLE BILL AND AUNT ROSE

Uncle Bill was of a comical nature. Aunt Rose, on the other hand, was stern. She did, however, enjoy his harmonica playing, and would often sing along, even if a little off-key.

In the late 1980's or early 1990's, Uncle Bill and Aunt Rose made their final trip to Krebs. At this time, Aunt Rose was suffering from dementia, or early Alzheimers. Uncle Bill wanted her to see her siblings one more time. Her behavior at this time was very uncharacteristic of her. She cursed and swore at Uncle Bill, even attempting to strike him at times. At other times, her behavior was quite normal. It was very upsetting to my dad, who felt they should not have made the trip at all. Shortly after their return to Ohio, Aunt Rose passed on. Uncle Bill continued on for some time, but his mind also began to falter. He later deteriorated to a point where he could not speak, and sometimes did not recognize his relatives.

I distinctly recall the final time I saw Uncle Bill. It was around the year 1996. I had traveled up to Akron, Ohio, along with my wife, Connie, daughter Carolyn, Uncle Angelo, and cousin James Scarpitti. We had recently purchased a late model Ford Aerostar Van, and the ride was quite comfortable. We made a two-day trip to attend Uncle Scrip and Aunt Louise's 50th wedding anniversary. It was a grand celebration, with music provided by Dick Massaro and his band. He was Uncle Bill and Aunt Rose's son, and an accomplished accordion player. Uncle Bill was there in his wheel chair, brandishing his usual bright smile, beneath the little moustache. Family members even had him dancing around in his wheel chair. He loved the music, as always. When he saw me, he gave me an intense look and a smile. Only one word came out.

"Oklahoma."

I realized that he had made the connection.

Shortly after this grand celebration, Uncle Bill returned to his beloved Rose. This generation of Scarpittis was beginning to fade away.

CHAPTER 7

UNCLE ORLAND AND AUNT MARY

(Uncle Orland and Aunt Mary in their young years. They are standing in front of the Pulchny home located next to our old home place that burned. This rock house is still in good condition today. This photo was likely taken before children came along.)

Uncle Orland and Aunt Mary, also, made the trip to Krebs each summer to spend a week or so with my Grandparents. They had two daughters, Anna Marie and Christine. Uncle Orland was a stickler for getting an early start. So, about 4 am, the family had to be packed and ready to leave. As a child, I remember them driving an early model Chevrolet, 49 or 50 model. Of course, no air conditioners in those days, so the drive down could be a warm one. As usual, I would be at my grandparents' home awaiting their arrival. Usually Grandpa and I would be working in his garden. Soon we would hear the sound of a car engine. Excitedly, we would head for the porch near the road.

UNCLE ORLAND AND AUNT MARY

"Yep! Sure there is, boy! There is!"

The family would pile out of the car and we would give our welcoming hugs. Then Grandma would appear on the porch, and they raced to her open arms.

Uncle Orland was employed at a bus company in Akron for many years. His job was to clean and prepare the buses before they departed for their destinations. In this process, he would frequently discover items which travelers left behind. For the most part, these were often umbrellas. If they were not claimed at the bus station after a period of time, he could take them home. So, on most of his trips to Krebs, he provided us with much-needed umbrellas.

Aunt Mary was a fabulous cook. Soon, her and Grandma were preparing sauce for a delicious pasta supper. I usually hung around for this meal. My parents often wondered why I was not hungry at supper up on the hill. It was hard to tell them that I was already full of pasta!

As mentioned earlier, almost everyone in the neighborhood of eleven-and-a-half had nick-names. Uncle Orland was known as "Plooks". I never learned how he derived this name.

Uncle Orland was a lover of watermelon. Frequently he would have one in the car when he arrived. Sometimes, it would even be cold! If so, there would be a feast on the porch right away. Even choc beer would accompany this celebration. During his stay, he would often search out peddlers and return with two or three large melons.

UNCLE ORLAND AND AUNT MARY

During these early days, I always enjoyed times with my cousins, Anna Marie and Christine. We gathered on our Grandparents' porch in the shady afternoons. I was a little naïve. They had their way with me. I was frequently made up like a girl, lip stick, hair do, the works. It was all in fun, and we laughed heartily. The worse problem was removing that darn lipstick, not to mention the bobby pins stuck in my thick black hair.

There is a condition within the Scarpitti family which has become known as "The Scarpitti Syndrome", or even "The Scarpitti Curse". It is a mental condition which has descended down from Grandpa John's ancestry. It can take several forms, from clinical depression, schizophrenia, anxiety, even at times, frightening visions. It tends to afflict mainly the males in the family. It is not a retardation, as in the case of Uncle Cap, but is a condition which is sometimes treatable with psychiatric therapy and medication. From his youth, Uncle Orland was afflicted with this condition. My mom related this incident from his teen-age years.

When in high school, Uncle Orland dated a girl who lived in the neighborhood. She was of another group of Italian immigrants who were named "Ramzetti". Her family lived a few blocks away from my Grandparents' home. Uncle Orland decided to pay her a visit one evening. After having supper with she and her family, it had grown dark outside. He bid her good night and started to make his way back home. His path took him near the coal mining disaster described above. As he hurriedly walked along, he suddenly heard the sound of horse hooves behind him. He turned to see a white horse galloping toward him. It was carrying a headless man! Scared out of his wits, he ran as swiftly as possible all the way home, still hearing the galloping horse behind him. He raced up onto the porch and dashed into the dining room. He was completely breathless, and white as a ghost himself. He was in a daze. Grandpa grabbed him and shook him.

"OrLAND! OrLAND! What been happen you?"

It was some minutes before he caught his breath and described the horrific scene. I don't know if he visited that girlfriend again. If he did, I'm sure he took another route.

Christine was Uncle Orland's baby girl. He had a special name for her, a term of endearment. I have no idea where he derived this special name. To him, she was "Kooker-talley". I don't know if she ever took a special liking to this name or not.

I had the privilege of visiting the home of Uncle Orland and Aunt Mary in 1962, the year I graduated from high school. It was a stately home which Aunt Mary inherited from her parents. The home was two-story, with a full basement. The base boards were solid oak, and about 10 inches wide. Many of the antique furnishings were still present, and were fashioned from intricate wood. Aunt Mary treasured this home, as did Uncle Orland and the girls. On my visit, Aunt Mary was a gracious hostess. The delicious meals she prepared were great. She filled my plate, as well as Uncle Orland's, and set them before us. We were always asked if we wanted a second helping. The first was usually plenty for me. The bowls were large! This was followed by a delicious dessert which she also prepared. I'm sure this was a tradition handed on to her. The men were served first. When I visited many years later, nothing had changed. My food was set before me. The dessert followed. After that, I was instructed to retreat to the living room and relax. I always complied.

Uncle Orland served his country in the U. S. Army in World War II. I don't know if he ever saw action or not. I do know that he was very near it. Mom related an incident where he was driving a convoy truck, carrying supplies from one area to another. His was the last truck in the convoy. It was cold winter time, the heater on, and all windows rolled up. At one point, the convoy realized that he was not following along. One of the trucks turned around and retraced the route. A couple of miles back, the driver encountered Uncle Orland's truck at a stand-still, the engine running. He approached the truck to find him slumped over the steering wheel. He had suffered from carbon-monoxide poisoning. After some time, he recovered in the infirmary. I don't know if he saw more action after this, or if he was discharged. This occurrence probably did little good to help his mental condition. He continued to suffer episodes throughout his lifetime.

As related to me by cousin Anna Marie, Uncle Orland was a strict disciplinarian. As the girls approached their teenage years, it became a challenge for them to go out on a date in the evening. Uncle Orland would drill them. 'Who were they going out with? Where were they going? Was anyone else going along? A number of other questions followed. Then a curfew was set.

Anna Marie queried her mom about this more than once.

UNCLE ORLAND AND AUNT MARY

"My gosh, Mom! What did dad do when he was young?"

I don't know if Aunt Mary was ever able to give a reasonable explanation or not, but the questioning continued.

Like Grandpa John, Uncle Orland suffered greatly with his mental condition after his retirement. In his anguish, he began to feel that his life was useless, and that he was a burden on Aunt Mary and the family. Medication and psychiatric therapy did little good. One day he decided to end it all. He caught what he felt was an opportune time. Aunt Mary was out of the house for a time. He could take it no longer. He retreated down into the basement, gun in hand. He placed a chair in the middle of the floor. Then he spread newspapers all around. He sat in the chair, put the gun to his head, and pulled the trigger. It was the feast of the Annunciation of Mary, March 25, 1986. Uncle Orland went to join his parents, his siblings, in a land where mental illness is unknown, where even Uncle Cap enjoys mental health.

Aunt Mary returned home later to discover the horrific scene in the basement. I never learned whether there was a suicide note. I did learn of Aunt Mary's strength and spirit. She cleaned up the bloody basement. She and her daughters laid Uncle Orland to rest. Aunt Mary continued to live in her stately home following this tragedy. In later years, my wife Connie and I had the great honor of visiting her once again. She was the same pleasant, smiling Aunt Mary. The meals were prepared and set before us. The desserts followed. The relaxation in the living room continued. How strong she was! What an inspiration she was to all!

She continues to live today. She is no longer residing in the stately home. In her 90's now, she resides in a nursing home in the Akron area. I bet she's the same Aunt Mary, smiling, doing her best to fill the plates of the residents there, and placing them before them with a smile.

UPDATE: As I was formulating the final chapters of this book, I received the tragic news of the death of Aunt Mary. She passed in December of 2016, at the ripe old age of 98. May she rest in peace.

CHAPTER 8

UNCLE SCRIP AND AUNT LOUISE

(Above Uncle Scrip stands, his arm around brother Cap. Look at the hair! Notice the baseball glove in the foreground. Look closely. Part of an old model 30's car behind them)

Uncle Scrip undoubtedly was a lover of baseball. Before this photo was snapped, he was likely heading for the ball park. He had a great knowledge of the game, and was quite a skilled player. He and Aunt Louise and family, too, traveled to Krebs each summer for a visit. They had three children, Johnny, Sandra, and Marla. After a two-day trip, they would all be tired, but if there should happen to be a ball game going on in the park, Uncle Scrip would grab his glove and take off to the park. In those early days, my Dad would also sometimes be playing on the team. He was a skilled pitcher as well as an outfielder. Uncle Scrip would often fill a position in the outfield. If there had been major league scouts around eleven-and-a-half, these two may have been major leaguers.

Uncle Scrip's given name was Sylvester, 'Salvatore" in Italian. When I asked how he acquired this nick name, I was told that it came from his love for writing. Perhaps some of it rubbed off on me.

Uncle Scrip also served his country in World War II as a paratrooper in the U. S. Army. He fought in the Battle of the Bulge, and was wounded in a parachuting event, receiving a Purple Heart. After returning from the War, he married Aunt Louise 'Milazzo' on May 25, 1946, in Johnstown, Pennsylvania. They moved to Akron, Ohio a few months later and raised their three children.

I always enjoyed their summer time visits. Johnny was a few years younger than I, and while here I always had a fishing partner. We would grab our poles and head for the nearest pond or creek. On our journey to these fishing holes, we had to wade through weeds, brush, and thorn patches. I was more accustomed to this than Johnny. On one summer visit the chiggers were prolific. These little critters did not occur in Akron. We had quite a day and after cleaning the fish, we were already itching and scratching. I headed home for a bath. Johnny headed for Grandma's bath tub. Mom doctored all of my red itchy bites the best she could. Then I headed back over the hill to check on Johnny.

(Aunt Louise and Johnny when he was just a toddler)

Aunt Louise and Grandma had doctored Johnny up the best they could, covering his bites with anti-itch creams, but he was still scratching intensely at the red bites around his waist. That night I was told that he scratched and cried all night long. I could not persuade him to accompany me on another fishing trip that summer.

A summer or two later, Uncle Scrip and family were once again in Krebs for their annual visit. I had just turned 14 at the time. I had a girlfriend who lived in the town of Crowder, about 15 miles north of Krebs. To get there, I would walk over to 69 Highway, about a half-mile to the west. Here I would hitch a ride to Crowder. Imagine, 14 years old! Things were quite different in those early days. I decided on this particular day to go visit my girlfriend. My friend, Billy Jeff Miller, would accompany me. We started to make our way down the road when Johnny called from behind us.

"Hey! Where are you guys going?"

"We're going to Crowder to see my girlfriend." I replied.

"Can I come along?"

"Is it alright with Uncle Scrip?" I asked.

"Oh, sure. He don't care." Johnny said.

So, the three of us made our way to the highway. Before long an old gentleman stopped and gave us a ride to Crowder. He dropped us off in the town, and we made our way to my girlfriend's house. Her parents were home, of course. Otherwise, I never would have been invited. Along with a couple of other boys and girls, we walked to a nearby park, playing on the swings there. Later we walked to a nearby creek and tossed pebbles into the small clear stream. When evening drew near, we walked back to my girlfriend's house. Her parents had a chicken dinner prepared and we were invited to join them. By that time, it was growing late, and would soon be getting dark. We made our way back to the highway and soon caught a ride back to Krebs. As we were approaching Grandpa's house, I knew something was not right. Uncle Scrip was walking down the road toward us. He had a stern expression on his face.

He grabbed Johnny by the arm. "Where have you been, son? Your mom and I were worried sick about you."

Johnny only looked down. He did not respond. I decided to speak up.

UNCLE SCRIP AND AUNT LOUISE

"We've been to Crowder, Uncle Scrip. I went to see my girlfriend."

"Crowder? How did you get there?"

"We hitch-hiked. Johnny said you didn't care. It was ok with you."

"Oh, he did, did he? And you hitch-hiked?"

"Yeah, I do it all the time. Mom and Dad know about it. I'm sorry, Uncle Scrip. I thought you knew."

"It's alright Bill. It was not your fault."

He turned his attention to Johnny, who was still looking at his shoes. "I ought to bust you good! I never gave you permission to do this. Wait until your mom hears about this. There goes your privileges for this trip, buddy!"

He marched Johnny back to Grandpa's house. I hurriedly made my way back up the hill. I wanted to avoid what was coming for Johnny. He did not accompany me on any other ventures that summer. And, when my parents got wind of what happened, it was the end of my trips to Crowder.

Uncle Scrip and Mom were quite similar in looks and temperament. They were usually of a pleasant nature, but they could also be stern and strict if necessary. If they felt something needed to be said, it was done. Nothing was held back.

Uncle Scrip worked at Hamlin Metal Stamping Plant in Akron for many years. Here he derived another nickname, "Joe".

UNCLE SRIP AND AUNT LOUISE

Perhaps it was easier to remember than 'Scrip'. Here he was personnel manager until his retirement in 1984.

(Uncle Scrip in his later years. The resemblance to mom is striking, even the glasses)

In my later years, Aunt Louise shared an interesting story concerning her life with Uncle Scrip. His love for baseball was never-ending. Even when the family was young, he was constantly heading off to the ball park, either watching a game or playing in one. She remained at home tending to the house, and caring for the young family. One day she had had enough. Uncle Scrip was heading out for the ball park once again. She informed him that if he went to the ball park again, she and the kids would be gone when he got home. It did not dissuade him in the least. While he was gone, Aunt Louise packed her suit case, and those of the children. Then she headed for the bus station. While they were awaiting the arrival of the bus, she began to have second thoughts. Where would she go? What would she do with three small children, alone? They loved their father, and so did she! After all, he could be doing worse things. She returned home with the small children. The matter, as far as I know, was never discussed again. Son

UNCLE SCRIP AND AUNT LOUISE

Johnny followed in his dad's footsteps, loving the game of baseball, even being coached by his dad.

Uncle Scrip was very active in his community, coaching various little league teams, and adults as well. In the Hamlin Metal Plant where he was employed, he even coached a softball team for a group of challenged men who were employed there. Many of them were mutes, unable to speak or hear, communicating by signs! They developed a great love and respect for the man who offered his time and talents to them.

Uncle Scrip loved family, being with them, playing games with them. On one summer visit, he brought along a volley ball net and set it up between the two clothes-line poles in my grandparents' back yard. The whole family, children and adults participated in the game. Afterwards it was soda pop, water melon, and choc beer.

In the summer of 1962, I had just graduated from high school. My sister, Marilyn, her husband Jim, cousin Patricia, and I traveled to Akron for a visit. Jim drove his 1957 Ford. It was a two-day trip. We had a wonderful time visiting all of our relatives there, sharing great meals, and fellowship. After a few days, it was time to pack up and head back for Oklahoma. I had been talking to Uncle Scrip, and was encouraged to hang around for a while. He promised me a job at the Hamlin Plant, so I decided to take him up on the offer, to see what it would bring. At the time, I had just turned 18. I was placed on an assembly line where various metal parts were made. I was working with a woman machinist who was operating a large machine equipped with a die which came down swiftly, cutting metal brake shoes from thick sheets of metal. The woman knew how to operate that machine! Those metal parts were turned out pretty fast. My job was to grind down the rough edges using a machine equipped with a swiftly-turning sanding belt. I would grind them down and toss them into a nearby barrel. I could hardly keep up with the woman's speed. Uncle Scrip approached me.

"How's it going? Are you able to keep up?"

"Not very well, Uncle Scrip. That woman is really fast!"

"Well, I've got some news which might help you along. If you can keep up with her, the company has agreed to pay you the same salary she receives. How does that sound?"

I lit up with excitement. "Really? Boy, I'll do my best."

That woman was probably making over $3 per hour! That was good wages for a boy of 18. I worked with that woman for a couple of weeks, and I did keep up. My fingers and finger nails were ground down to nubs to show for it.

I enjoyed my stay with Uncle Scrip and his family that summer, but Ohio was not for me. Uncle Scrip had to go out and warm up the car before we went to work. This was July! I missed my family and friends back in Krebs. I did learn some lessons and values from Uncle Scrip, however. I was asked to pay a small fee for room and board, which was fine with me. Johnny and I slept in the attic where there were two beds for us, and a bathroom. Toward the end of that summer, though, I'd had enough. I took a train back to Oklahoma, and Krebs.

UNCLE SCRIP AND AUNT LOUISE

Uncle Scrip and his family continued making their visits to Krebs, and I always enjoyed their stays here. After many years, I returned to Akron for a special occasion. It was Uncle Scrip and Aunt Louise's 50th wedding anniversary in 1996. I had recently purchased a Ford Aerostar Van, which was comfortable traveling for the trip. Accompanying me were my wife, Connie, Uncle Angelo, cousin Jim, and our daughter, Carolyn. Uncle Angelo served as our g p s, knowing exactly where we needed to go. This was a grand celebration with good food, entertainment, and visiting. At one point the parish priest entered the room and found Uncle Scrip. I was standing nearby. He grabbed Uncle Scrip's arm.

"Hey, Scrip! What was the weather like 50 years ago?"

Uncle Scrip gave the priest a puzzled look. "The weather? Who was thinking about the weather?"

Everyone within hearing distance burst out in laughter.

About eight years later, I made another trip to Akron. It was in February, 2004. Uncle Scrip had returned to the Lord. My wife, Connie and I flew to Ohio to attend his funeral. He passed away on February 17, 2004, at the age of 83 years. He had developed cancer a few months before, which had metastasized into his vital organs, causing his death. Cousin Johnny related that he expressed to his dad that he would take him to M. D. Anderson Hospital in Houston for treatment. Uncle Scrip told him that he had lived to a ripe old age, and was content. He did not want to endure the pain and suffering which chemotherapy would bring upon him. He wanted to live life to the fullest until the end, and he did. A memorable event took place at his graveside before we laid him to rest. Johnny brought along a cd player and turned it on. Echoing throughout the area was Uncle Scrip's favorite song..."Take Me Out to the Ballgame". We could not hold back the tears. An image entered my mind, a vision of Uncle Scrip in center field, and my Dad on the pitcher's mound. Dad had passed away only three years before.

Aunt Louise lived for about five more years. She did not remain at home for long, finding it too lonesome without her beloved Scrip. She soon moved in with her daughter Sandy, and remained with her until her death in July of 2009. The generation of Scarpittis were growing fewer in number.

CHAPTER 9

UNCLE ANGELO AND AUNT MARY ANN

(In the above photo, Uncle Angelo stands on the porch of his home, my Mom standing near him.)

Uncle Angelo was the baby of the Scarpitti siblings. My Mom recalled the day he was born. In those early times, there were few doctors available to deliver babies. This was mostly up to mid-wives who lived in the area. One such mid-wife lived in the neighborhood. She was a cousin of Grandpa John, in the

Sellers family. When it was near time for Grandma Concetta to give birth, she was summoned. Grandpa John chased all the kids out of the house, telling them to go out doors and play. Grandma Concetta could be heard wailing aloud in the house as she labored to give birth. Soon there was the sound of a baby crying. In a few moments, Grandpa John appeared on the porch.

"Hey! You got the baby broth'! Come, look! Boy, sure he's fat!"

Mom and her siblings rushed into the bed room to get their first glimpse of their baby brother. In his infancy and his toddler years, it became the duty of Mom and Aunt Rose to help care for him. Not many baby buggies were available at the time, or perhaps one could not be afforded. At any rate, when Grandma Concetta walked to the grocery store a few blocks away, Mom and Aunt Rose would often be employed to carry Uncle Angelo, and even Uncle Scrip, who at the time, was also small. Mom often related how they would have to stop from time to time to give their arms a rest.

From his early years, Uncle Angelo was regarded as pretty bright by his family. However, he too, was afflicted by the Scarpitti Sndrome. Mom related how it became obvious as he approached his teenage years. Sometimes, even while in high school, he would retreat to his bedroom for a day or more, seldom coming out, even to eat. After graduating from high school, he was the only one of his siblings who attended college. He spent a couple of years at Eastern State College in Wilburton, Oklahoma. This was the time when the mental affliction hit him the hardest, and he did not graduate.

He grew up in the neighborhood of eleven-and-a-half, and became attracted to a beautiful young girl nearby, Mary Ann Dominic. She was the daughter of Shoe Peg and Thresa.

(Uncle Angelo and Aunt Mary Ann before marriage and children. The old car may have been his.)

After they were married, they lived with Aunt Mary Ann's parents for a time. Shortly later they moved a few blocks away and rented a portion of Chick Sellers home where they remained for a number of years. They later had three children...Patricia, Jim, and Lawrence.

Across the street from them lived a large woman by the name of Mrs. Blevins. She and her son, Butch, rented an old small shack that also belonged to Chick Sellers. Mrs. Blevins was not known to bathe very often! When she was around, the stench was almost unbearable. Occasionally she would wander across the street to pay a visit to Aunt Mary Ann. She was a neat freak. Her house was always immaculately clean. As soon as Mrs. Blevins would leave, Aunt Mary Ann would grab some disinfectant spray and a rag to clean the chair where Mrs. Blevins sat. Patricia was small at the time, but soon picked up on this. Following a subsequent visit, Mrs. Blevins was going out the door to her shack. Patricia raced to her mom.

"Ma, hurry, get the rag! The chair really stinks!"

I'm sure Mrs. Blevins heard this, but it did not dissuade her from future visits. I had the pleasure of attending grade school at St. Joseph's with her son, Butch! He also exuded a somewhat unpleasant odor, so most kids did their best to avoid him.

As the children began to grow, Uncle Angelo had a home built a few blocks away. It is located over the hill to the east of our old home place. Here, he and Aunt Mary Ann raised their family.

In her youth, Aunt Mary Ann was a strikingly beautiful young woman. There were a number of gentlemen who expressed the desire to marry her. She, however, always had eyes for her beloved Angelo. They grew up only a block or so away from one another, yet they ended up together for many years.

Aunt Mary Ann was stern, but also gentle, and generous hearted. She was a devout Catholic, attending daily Mass, and even providing transportation to women in the area who needed a way to Mass. Following Mass, she would deliver them again to their homes. Cousin Jim, her son, would often accompany her and the ladies to daily Mass.

Aunt Mary Ann loved salads, topped with her own home-made dressing. In the spring time, there was a type of wild lettuce which grew in the area known as "checotahs". I don't know if there is any connection with this and the town of Checotah located about 40 miles to the north. Aunt Mary Ann could often be seen during this time of the year, knife in hand, as she searched through nearby fields for this delicacy.

During these times, they usually had their supper around 4 or 4:30 in the afternoon. On the other hand, mom usually had ours around 5:30 or so. Without fail, as we were finishing our supper, Aunt Mary Ann would appear at the door.

"Do yous' have any salad left?"

She would grab the bowl from the table and a fork and polish off the rest of the salad. Mom also created a tasty salad, using her own recipe.

Even in her youth, Aunt Mary Ann was known for her love and generosity. During Easter time, she knew of some poor neighborhood children, who may not be provided with Easter baskets, or eggs. At her own expense, she supplied baskets, dyed Easter eggs, and promoted an Easter egg hunt for these children.

When my sisters Marilyn and Phyllis were small girls, Aunt Mary Ann sometimes had a small chore for them. She would appear up on the hill, especially in the summer time. She then summoned them to a nice shade tree outdoors. Here she supplied a razor and a pan of water. Then the command.

"You girls, shave my legs for me!"

I don't know if there was anything in this for my sisters. Perhaps this is how they learned to shave their own legs.

(Uncle Angelo and Aunt Mary Ann in later years)

When I was approaching puberty, like most kids of this age, I developed a form of acne. Fortunately, the unsightly bumps appeared on my back, not my face. Aunt Mary Ann became aware of this. She would sometimes come up to our home on the hill. I could not hide from her. She always searched me out.

"Billy, come here! Take your shirt off!"

I always complied. It was useless to argue with her. I took a seat in a chair outdoors under the shade tree. Then the unpleasant task began. She was always equipped with a bottle of alcohol! The juicy bumps were squeezed from my back. Then the alcohol was applied as a disinfectant. I screamed in agony. Aunt Mary Ann always had something to say.

"Oh, Billy, hush! It can't burn that bad!"

With tear-filled eyes, I grabbed my shirt and headed back into the house.

Although Aunt Mary Ann was as neat as a pin, she was not afraid to dirty her hands. During the special hog-butchering days, it was always her duty to strip the intestines. These were cleaned and later used for casings for the famous Italian sausage. The process was messy and smelly. This never seemed to bother her in the least.

In later years, after his family was grown, Uncle Angelo's battle with the Scarpitti Syndrome intensified. He was likely in his late 50's at this time. He was living in his home with Aunt Mary Ann, Patricia, and mother-in-law, Thresa. He suffered from severe depression, and other afflictions. He often made a statement to them.

"I'm just like my dad. I'm useless. I'm going to die young."

They all tried to convince him that he was still young. Grandpa died when he was 72. But, it was all in vain to Uncle Angelo. Finally, his suffering became unbearable for him and the family. He fell a couple of times in the house. Even he himself realized that something had to be done. He was soon entered into the mental hospital in Vinita, Oklahoma, where other family members had once been admitted. He did not protest, realizing that this might be beneficial. He remained here for some months. I accompanied Aunt Mary Ann a couple of times to pay him a visit. After some treatment and medications, he was allowed to return home. However, he did not want to remain in his home with the family. He felt he would do better in isolation, living alone. Consequently, he moved into my grandparents' old home and modified it to suit his needs, even making it smaller by removing two of the rooms. Here he remained until later years.

In the meantime, Aunt Mary Ann, her mom Thresa, and Patricia remained in the family home. After a few years, Thresa passed away, leaving Patricia and her mom alone in the house. The boys, Jim and Lawrence, were married and out of the home. Lawrence lived nearby. Jim had moved to Tulsa. He later told me that when he visited, he never left for home until a nice goodie bag was packed for him. She cared greatly for her children.

After a few years, Aunt Mary Ann became ill and underwent colon surgery, receiving a colostomy. During this time of recovery, Patricia took good care of her mom. Miraculously, after some months the colostomy was reversed, a rare occurrence. After some time, Aunt Mary Ann began to fail, but remained at home under the care of Patricia. When this became no longer possible, she spent a short time in a nursing home before her death. Her 'humor' and disposition remained the same. If something was on her mind, she didn't hesitate to tell you. Shortly before her death I visited her in the nursing home. She looked at me rather disgustedly.

"Bill, you need a haircut!"

I'm sure if there was a clipper around, she would have gone to work.

When I visited, it was January, a couple of weeks after Christmas. A Santa Claus was still hanging on her door. She expressed her frustration.

"I wish they'd take that damn Santa Claus down!"

It is easy for me to remember the day Aunt Mary Ann entered heaven. It occurred on Connie and I's 20th wedding anniversary. She was laid to rest on January 18, 2003, just one day before her 80th birthday. Aunt Mary Ann lived a rich full life.

Uncle Angelo continued living in the old home place alone. Patricia went down frequently to tend to his various needs, washing dishes and laundry, cooking, and cleaning. After two or three years, his health also began to fail, and he entered into an assisted living center, where he could be looked after more intensely. Again, he lived in his own small apartment, and his meals were prepared for him, and all his needs were provided. A couple of years before his death, he developed a cancer in one of his legs, which later metastasized to other areas of his body, lungs and kidneys. When he could no longer remain in the assisted living center, he was transferred to a nursing facility, Walnut Grove Living Center in south McAlester. The last month or so of his life was lived out here. He remained under Hospice care until his death on February 17, 2010. He passed only four months after Mom who died on October 30, 2009. Ironically, he occupied the very same room where Mom stayed when she was at the same Center. He passed in the very same room, in the very same bed, as our dear Mom. I suppose she wanted her baby brother in heaven with her. Uncle Angelo always felt like he would die relatively young. He was wrong. He out-lived all of his brothers, reaching the ripe old age of 86. That generation of Scarpittis had passed over to their new heavenly homes. I've often wondered if there are beautiful large gardens there. Hopefully, there are no coal mines there, or if so, perhaps they are explosion-proof!

CHAPTER 10

MOM AND DAD

(Photo of Mom and Dad, probably in their 60's)

Mom and Dad were a special blend of full-blood Italian, and practically full-blood Irish. Arguments could become very heated at times. But, there was a very genuine love which developed in their teenage years which held everything together. A marriage which everyone thought would do well to last only a couple of months, thrived for nearly 66 years! They became infatuated with one another at a very early age. Mom attended the Catholic

MOM AND DAD

school; Dad attended the Krebs Public School, but somehow, they connected. Perhaps it was their love for the game of baseball. Dad was a talented player, even in little league. Mom was an enthusiastic spectator. Perhaps they met at one of his games. At any rate, at an early age they met at the Krebs Public School ground. If Dad had a few coins in his pocket, he would escort mom to the drug store and treat her to her favorite ice cream.

Dad learned to become independent at a very early age. His Mom passed when he was just six months old, and his Dad passed when he was only about 12 years old. For a few years, he was cared for by his grandmother and an aunt. His older brother, Uncle Smokey, was already grown and on his own. Dad and his middle brother, Uncle Gene, a couple of years older than he, remained with these two women for a time. Dad was rather turned off to religion at an early age. Here is the reason. He related how his grandmother and aunt were of different religious beliefs. During the wee hours of the night, they could be heard shouting and arguing about which religion was the true one. Dad and Uncle Gene would have to cover their heads with pillows to drown out the noise. No wonder they never wanted to attend a Sunday School!

While they were quite young, Uncle Smokey and Uncle Gene moved to Oakley, California, where they went to work. This was not far from San Francisco. Here they remained, raising their families. Dad remained behind, living near what was known as "Painters' Mountain", thus called because it was occupied by some of his Painter relatives. His grandmother was a Painter. As a child, I recall visiting this area a few times where my Dad had an uncle by the name of Joe Painter. We would have picnics here at times, and even shoot off fireworks on the 4th of July. Woods and a sizeable creek nearby provided good hunting and fishing.

(Dad's grandparents on the Painter side. His mother was their daughter. Notice the bright smiles!)

Dad spoke of his grandfather as being a preacher. I never learned what denomination he belonged to. If I were to make a guess, it would probably be Baptist. I'm sure they were among the first to settle upon Painter Mountain. They were likely laid to rest at the Red Oak Cemetery, located just north of Bache, Oklahoma. However, their graves are no longer marked. I never learned what work Dad's grandfather did. I know that he was not a coal miner. Most likely he was either a rancher or farmer, or perhaps some of each. This seemed to be the chief occupation during those early times.

(Dad's parents, Wesley and Margaret Anderson. Look at the black hat and the moustache. Doesn't he look like an outlaw? And his mom with the big white hat. Notice who is sitting! But, she almost has a smile.)

Dad never spoke much about his parents. I suppose it was just too painful for him. It seems I recall him saying that his dad did work in the coal mine for a short time. One event I recall was he related that his dad spent some time in jail once. I don't know why. It could have been boot-legging during those times. Dad recalled when the sheriff came to arrest him. He reassured them.

"Don't worry, kids. I'll be home in a little while."

Dad's parents are both buried at the Red Oak Cemetery at Bache. Their graves are in separate areas, but they are marked. His mom died in 1915. His dad passed a number of years later. Dad was always faithful to decorate their graves on each

MOM AND DAD   121

Memorial Day. He took a hoe and rake to clean around their graves and their stones. Then he placed wreaths lovingly near their stones. He never once failed to pay them tribute in this way.

(Above is a real gem. Dad and brother, Uncle Gene. Dad must have been only around 5 or 6 at this time, and it had to be winter. Look at the heavy coats, and the smiles. Perhaps they were going out to play in the snow!)

Dad and his brothers were always close, since they lost everything at such an early age. In later times when his brothers would come to visit from California, there was always a lot of fishing and choc beer drinking. There was a great deal of socializing and fun times. These are times that are forever etched into my memory. Uncle Gene would always drive up, a big wide smile on his face.

Dad and Uncle Gene were both baseball lovers. In earlier times, Dad related how Uncle Gene was a good catcher. He would often pitch while his brother caught. After these years were all behind them, Uncle Gene still had the scars. The fingers and knuckles, especially on his right hand, were all bent and crooked. As a small boy, I asked him about this once.

"Uncle Gene, why are your fingers so crooked?"

He gave me that wide smile. "You know when someone's trying to steal second base? That's from trying to get the ball out of the mitt too fast!"

In other words, when he was catching, if a runner on first base was trying to steal second, he would try to throw the ball before it was even caught in the mitt! No wonder the crooked, broken fingers!

Uncle Gene also loved to fish, but he hated snakes. I distinctly recall one fishing trip I took him on when he was visiting Krebs. This was when he was in his early 50's. There was a great pond I knew of in the Stuart, Oklahoma area. It was owned by a friend of mine, who allowed me to drive through the gate, cross a small creek, and drive right up to the pond. It was stocked with large black bass, one of his favorites. It was also stocked with big water moccasins. We remained near the truck for a while, and caught a few small bass, using minnows for bait. Uncle Gene started to walk to the other side. Suddenly he shouted out.

"There's a snake over here!"

He continued to make his way around to the other side of the pond. Soon he screamed out again.

"Hey! There's another snake, a big one."

I hollered back. "Maybe you better come back over here."

A few more steps and he yelled again. "I'll be damn! Here's another damn snake! Maybe we better find another pond."

I managed to convince him to stay, and we did come home with a nice stringer of bass to show for our efforts. And neither of us was bitten by a snake!

I enjoyed a lot of good times with my uncles, Smokey and Gene when they visited us in Krebs. From my childhood into my adult years these memories continue to be treasured. One event particularly stands out. It probably took place in the late 60's. It was a time, rarely, when Uncle Gene and Uncle Smokey were both here at the same time. My brother, Sonny, and I had placed a trot line in Lake Eufaula a few miles north of Krebs. One day when Sonny was at work, the two uncles and I decided to check that trot line. The boat we were using was a small aluminum v bottom, with a tiny hand-cranked motor which was a bit cantankerous to start at times. Finally, Uncle Smokey got it running, and we slowly made our way across the lake to see if we had any fish on. The trot line was marked by white gallon jugs, the main line being submerged so boaters would not sever it. To raise the main line up, there was a large gaff hook in the bow of the boat. This was where Uncle Gene was positioned. When we arrived near the jug, he plunged the gaff hook into the water to raise the main line. He grabbed the line with the other hand, and tossed the gaff hook back to me. I was seated in the middle. The waters echoed with a loud scream.

(The trot line fishermen, from left, Sonny, Uncle Gene, Uncle Smokey, and dad)

"OOOWWUUUUCH!"

Looking in front of me, I soon found the problem. In tossing the gaff hook to me by the handle, Uncle Gene had somehow managed to imbed the large hook into the top of his hand. There he sat, main line in one hand, and the handle of the gaff hook in the other.

"Bill, pull that damn hook out!"

"Are you kidding? That big hook is imbedded in your hand past the barb. There's no way I can do it."

"Then, take a knife and cut it out!"

In the meantime, Uncle Smokey was sitting in the back, calmly waiting to see what the outcome would be.

"When was the last time you had a tetanus shot?" I asked.

"Hell, I don't know. Just pull the damn thing out."

"I can't do that. You better let that line go. We need to go to the emergency room and get it taken out."

Reluctantly, he finally agreed.

Uncle Smokey was calm, as usual. It took a great deal to excite him. He only smiled, as he struggled to get the old boat motor going again. Then, we slowly made our way back to the boat ramp. Meanwhile, Uncle Gene was grimacing as he held the handle of the gaff hook as still as possible, trying to keep the large hook from moving around too much.

"This is embarrassing as hell." He protested, as we loaded into my car, heading for the emergency room. The road was quite rough, so I did not drive very fast, trying in vain to not jostle the gaff handle.

Finally, we arrived at the emergency room, where I dropped Uncle Gene off at the entrance. It was a sight, as he emerged from the back seat, holding the gaff hook with his right hand.

"Oh, Hell! This is just too damn embarrassing!" He shouted again as we entered the emergency room.

"Oh, Uncle Gene! I'm sure they've seen worse things than this." I assured him.

"Hell! I doubt it!"

At this time, I was employed as a med tech at the McAlester Clinic. I was acquainted with all the doctors and even surgeons. It was our lucky day! One of the surgeons I knew well was there, Dr. Bill Blanchard. He removed the large hook and had the nurse administer a tetanus shot and bandage up the wound. More embarrassment followed when we drove to Mom and Dad's house with Uncle Gene's bandaged hand, and no fish!

Mom and Dad were married on March 2, 1935, but the story of getting to that point, according to Mom, was quite a challenge. Grandpa John never approved of their courtship. They tried to hide it from him, but he was aware due to the tongue-wagging of neighbors. One day while he and Shoe-peg were making their way to the old Columbus Lodge, Grandpa saw Mom and Dad walking along the road, holding hands. Nothing was said at the time. Everyone continued on their way. Dad was a young man at the time, around 18 years old. He knew of Grandpa John's dislike of him, and he became frightened, especially of what he may do to his daughter, Mary. As they were making their way along, he expressed his feelings to Mom. What she said surprised him.

"I've had enough of this! When Papa gets home, we're going to go talk to him."

Dad could not believe what he was hearing. "Oh, no! I'm not going down there! He'll kill me!"

"I don't think so." Said Mom. "He's got to know how we feel about each other."

Reluctantly, Dad went to the house to visit Grandpa. Mom related just how pleasant Grandpa John was to him, offering him choc beer, Italian sausage, and cheese. It was like he welcomed him with open arms. Dad could not believe his eyes. He felt at home, and comfortable. But, for whatever reason, it was all staged.

Later that evening, Dad bade farewell to everyone and started his walk back to Painter Mountain. That's when all hell broke loose! No sooner had Dad walked out the door when Grandpa John approached Mom. She was 19 at the time! Imagine!

"Sure as hell, you never see thata' boy 'gain! He no good! He lazy bum. He no good for you"

Mom could not believe what she was hearing. "Papa! What do you mean? Why did you treat him so good? Why did you give him choc and food, and now you hate him?"

MOM AND DAD

"He no good! Lazy boy."

"I don't know where you heard that." Mom protested. "He works all day long in the hayfield, in the hot sun, for 75 cents! How can you say he's lazy?"

"Never mind! You no see him 'gain!"

Mom, full blood Italian, a 19 year- old girl, stood her ground.

"I don't care what you say! Chester is a good boy, and I love him. Furthermore, if he asks me to marry him, I will."

Grandpa John turned red with rage. He reached back and gave Mom a sharp slap on the cheek. Without a further word, he retreated to his bedroom. The rest is history.

Mom and Dad eloped, and were married by a Justice of the Peace in Wilburton, Oklahoma. They stayed with some of Dad's relatives for a period of time. Mom was allowed to visit her parents, but Dad had to stay far away. He could remain outside the gate of the yard, but was not permitted to enter the property.

Grandpa John was still furious. "Sure, I get the gun!"

This situation lingered for a good year. All the while, Grandpa John had a plan which no one was aware of. He began to realize that perhaps Dad was not the bum he thought him to be. He saw his hard work, and his love for Mom. On the following Easter Sunday, 1936, Dad was welcomed into the family. Following this difficult trial period, he and Grandpa John became dear friends, even working side-by-side in the coal mine. They grew to love and respect one another.

MOM AND DAD

Grandpa John, even though tough at times, had a caring and generous heart. He realized Mom and Dad had a rough start. Consequently, he donated the old home place on the hill to them to give them a start. This is where me and my siblings grew up. The house consisted of a small kitchen and dining room along with two bedrooms. The larger bedroom Dad later partitioned off to make two smaller rooms. The one in the middle was shared by my brother and I. The one on the end, facing east, was occupied by my two sisters. There were not many furnishings....an old round coal stove in the dining room, a small kitchen table, a heavy round oak dining table, and three old heavy beds. There was virtually no closet space, and little room

for chest of drawers. My brother and I had no closet. The two sisters sectioned off a corner of their room for a small closet. Mom and Dad did the same in their small bedroom. Nonetheless, the family was compact, warm, well-fed, and happy.

(Here Marilyn stands in front of Dad's old 51 Chevrolet, March, 1959. In the background, a portion of the old home place, the window of our parents' bedroom facing south. Marilyn was 21 years young!)

Marilyn was the first little dumpling to come along, the apple of Dad's eye. She was born on November 28, 1937. She was chubby, with much black hair. In her toddler years, as she began to speak, she observed Dad, a glass of choc beer in his hand. She would look up at him.

"Me choc beer too, Dad! Me choc beer too!"

Dad always obliged by pouring a tiny bit of cold choc into a small glass.

Marilyn was always a great 'big sister' to me when I was growing up. She was always protective of me, and also did her best to help discipline me when it was necessary. I specifically recall one incident when I received a Daisy BB Gun for Christmas. I was 8 or 9 years old. My brother, Sonny and I, thought it would be fun to shoot birds in the tree below the old shanty. She immediately ran to Mom.

"Mama, Bill and Sonny are shooting birds by the shanty! Those poor birds aren't hurting anyone! Stop them!"

Believe me! Mom put a stop to that right away. Shooting squirrels and rabbits to eat was one thing. Shooting innocent birds was another.

Another incident involving Marilyn occurred when I was about 5 years old. She had gotten a bicycle, I believe for Christmas. She decided to take me for a ride. She placed me in front of her and we took off down the hill. As we approached the bottom, we lost control and the bike ran into the ditch, one of the handle bars hit me in the chest.

"Oh, my heart! My heart!" I screamed. "You hurt my heart!"

Marilyn only laughed. "I don't think it's your heart. You only bruised your chest."

"I'm going to tell mom anyway." I cried, as I made my way back to the house.

After Mom took a quick look at my chest, she also laughed. I felt neglected, but soon got over it, and was soon back on the bike with Marilyn.

(Phyllis and Raymond, her future husband, stand near our old house on the west side, May, 1959. Phyllis was 19 years young.)

During these early times, the bathroom was about 50 feet north of the old house. It was a two-seater! Marilyn was never afraid of anything, or anyone. When necessary, at night, she got out of bed and trekked to the outhouse, flashlight in hand. Phyllis, on the other hand, was scared of her own shadow! If she needed to go at night, someone had to go with her. If she could not persuade Marilyn to get out of bed, she always picked on me. To speak the truth, I was a bit devilish. Phyllis, being so afraid at night, did not want to make the entire trip to the outhouse. I held the flashlight while she squatted near the pear tree, about half-way. I waited until her pants were down and she was squatting. Then I took the flashlight and ran for the house. I laughed as Phyllis screamed, all the while pulling up her pants and running for the house.

"Just wait! I'm going to tell Mama."

I don't recall her ever telling Mom. I believe she was too afraid to wake her in the middle of the night.

We enjoyed many happy and adventurous times growing up on Anderson Hill, which I have come to name it. We were poor in some ways, but rich in what really mattered. We had two parents who we never doubted loved us. Dad, a poor coal miner, provided well for his family. There was never a time when there were not three meals a day on the table. Mom never worked outside the home. She would never have had time. Cleaning, doing laundry, and cooking for all of us was a full-time job. There were no fast-food restaurants in those times, and if there were we could never have afforded the luxury. Occasionally, a peddler may come by, selling watermelons, peaches, or cantaloupes. If Mom had an extra dollar, we might receive a special treat. A special name comes to mind, "Chew-tobacco". He drove a

MOM AND DAD

beat-up old pickup truck, had a speech impediment, and always had a wad of tobacco in his cheek. But, he always gave us a good deal on his produce. Occasionally, Dad might have a couple of extra bucks. An old Hispanic gentleman would come around, peddling his home-made tamales. They were delicious, and Dad would frequently patronize him. He drove an old gray Dodge Pickup truck, and he went by the name of "Hot Tamale Joe".

These were special treats for us growing up on the hill. Soda pop was also a treat, something we didn't have every day. Dad bought a six-pack of Pepsi on Saturdays, which we were treated with on our Sunday dinner. Cookies and other sweets were treated the same way. Again, I was known to be a little villain at times. I searched the kitchen. Sometimes, I grabbed a handful of cookies and darted out of the kitchen, hoping not to be seen. Sometimes it worked. Sometimes it didn't. I was often caught out in the yard by one of my sisters.

"You're not supposed to have those cookies. They're for tomorrow. I'm going to tell Mama."

I held onto the cookies for dear life. "If I can't have these cookies, no one is going to get them!"

I crumbled the cookies up in my hand, and they became chicken feed. When Mom or Dad found out about it, I, too, wished I were chicken feed!

Speaking of chickens, again, almost everyone in Krebs had a chicken yard. We were no exception. There was a sizeable chicken yard behind the shanty, and east of the outhouse. It was fenced in, of course. But sometimes, in the evening, the gate was opened so that the chickens could graze for a time in the yard. This could eliminate some of the bug problem. The problem was getting those blasted chickens back through the gate into the pen. Seems they could easily find their way out, but when being corralled, they could not find their way back in. It was frustrating, chasing them along the fence as they ran past the gate a number of times, clucking all the while! After their grazing in the yard, we never wanted to lose our chewing gum in the grass. It could easily be mistaken for chicken poop!

Regarding the chicken farming, a memorable event comes to mind. My brother, Sonny, and I, had special chores to do when we arrived home from school. We brought in kindling and coal in the winter time, and took turns feeding the chickens. I was probably in the fourth grade when I arrived home from school one day. It was a beautiful afternoon in the springtime. I was anxious to grab my fishing pole and head for the nearest pond or creek. For some reason, Dad was home early from the mine that day. I rushed to the bedroom to put on my fishing clothes. As I was rushing out the kitchen door, he grabbed my arm.

"Where are you going?"

"I'm going to five pond to catch some perch." I replied.

"Well, you go feed the chickens first."

"But, Dad!" I protested. "It's not my turn. It's Sonny's."

"I didn't ask you who the hell's turn it was! I told you to go feed the chickens."

MOM AND DAD

Disgustedly, I tossed my fishing pole on the ground, and hurried to the shanty. I grabbed the large coffee can and filled it with the corn scratch. Then I dashed to the chicken yard, opened the gate, and the clucking chickens started running toward me, realizing that it was feeding time. 'I'm going to get back to Dad', I thought. I grabbed handfuls of the hard scratch and tossed it as hard as possible at the chickens, striking them in the head and eyes. They shook their heads, and blinked in terror as they darted away from me. Satisfied with my accomplishment, I hurried to the shanty with the empty can. Then I made my way back to the house. I opened the kitchen door. Dad was standing in front of me, an angry look on his face.

"Boy, how would you like to have your food thrown at you like that?"

All the while Dad was watching from the kitchen window without my being aware of his vigilance. I knew I was in deep trouble. The coal miner's hand swatted my behind several times.

"Now, you're not going to any damn five pond today. In fact, you're not going all week. Go to your bedroom and think about what you did to the chickens. Maybe I'll let you have supper after a while, if you're lucky."

I never threw hard corn at the chickens again!

Another event of these early times is one which I shall never forget. It is forever etched into my mind. Today it would probably be regarded as child-abuse. As a little boy, I had a bad habit of not washing my hands before coming to the supper table. Dad had warned me about this on several occasions, but for some reason, I could not remember. Perhaps I was too hungry, and Mom prepared delicious food. So, came one evening at the supper table. I was probably around eight years old. We all sat down to eat. Dad looked at me.

"Boy, show me those hands."

Sheepishly, I raised my dirty hands for his inspection.

He took one look and jerked me from the table.

"It looks like I'm going to have to teach you to wash your hands before you eat. I've warned you too many damn times."

There was utter silence at the supper table as he escorted me outside to the 'little shanty'. It was located near the coal pile. It was dark outside. He placed me inside in darkness and locked the door behind him as he returned to the house.

"Hopefully, this will teach you to come to the table with clean hands." He said, as he made his way back to the house.

I was scared, and I cried as I waited for supper to finish, and for someone to unlock the door. Before long I heard footsteps approaching and the door unlatched. It was Mom. She hugged me and wiped the tears away. She escorted me back to the kitchen where a warm plate awaited me. Dad had retreated to the dining room, where he was reading the newspaper. I don't know if he knew or not, but Mom never failed to take care of her baby. She looked at me tenderly.

"Your Dad loves you. He doesn't want to be mean. He just wants you to be clean at supper. He's afraid you'll get sick."

MOM AND DAD

During the early to mid-50's polio was becoming rampant everywhere. Many people, including Dad, had the misconception that this disease was caused by uncleanliness, which explained his extraordinary means to discipline me. I never came to the supper table without spotless hands again. He taught me a lesson.

(A picture of the handsome me when I was around 13 or 14 years old. Notice all the wavy black hair and the gorgeous smile. Too far back! I can't remember if the girls were chasing me or not. They could probably find me at my favorite fishing spot!)

Unfortunately, I did contract polio a few years later, when I was eleven years old. It was caused by a virus, not dirty hands, which my Dad also learned. I was fortunate in that my case was mild. Some of my friends at the time became severely crippled, or worse. My case involved the instep of the left foot. About 70 to 80% of the muscle had been taken, resulting in complete loss of the arch, even callousing where the arch should be. Today, I wear an ankle brace on the left side, and a wedge in the shoe to support the arch. More of this story will be related later on.

Speaking of the little shanty mentioned above, another

(Here they are! One on each side of me. This was Marilyn's High School Graduation, May of 1956. I was a lad of 12 years old. Phyllis, on the left, would have been about 16 years old. This was on the east side of the old home place. Dad's garden is in background.)

adventure worthy of relating, although not one of my favorites, should be included. At the time, I probably had the hairiest legs of any boy in Krebs. Here's why. I would sometimes be escorted

MOM AND DAD   139

to this small building by my two older sisters. Mom was not aware of it. My pant legs were rolled up. Then the fun began. They produced a razor and a pan of warm soapy water. The water was rubbed onto my legs, and then the shaving began. I believe this is how my two sisters practiced as they began shaving their own legs. Luck for them ran out. One day the shanty door screeched open. To their horror, there stood mom with a horrified look on her face. The pan and the razor were escorted to the house, along with my two sisters. Their practicing days were finished. My legs never returned to normal.

Speaking of gardens, Dad had one of the finest in Krebs. He was a meticulous gardener, raising a large one during those days before tillers were available. Like Grandpa, his was done with spade and shovel. He also used one of the old-time push plows with the large wheel in front. After a day in the coal mine, he, too would toil in the garden until dark. He raised a variety of delicious vegetables. His garden was meticulously clean, no weeds, grass, or clutter. Rows were perfectly straight, with enough room between for cultivating.

(Dad in July, 1960. He was 45 years old. In his hand, I'm sure, is a can of beer. He was seldom seen without this, or a cold glass of choc beer. This was shortly before his mining accident in the winter of that year.)

Dad was not a big man, but he was stout and muscular, one who did not take a lot of crap from anyone. He could be very tender-hearted, or he could be someone you did not want to contend with when he became angry. He dealt with all of we, his children, in this manner, and we all learned to love and respect him for this.

When we were growing up on Anderson Hill, we looked at Dad as a big kid at heart. So many times, he shared in our fun. There are so many incidents worth relating that I hardly know where to begin. During the summers, he frequently took us swimming at one of the local ponds located near Alderson. It was known as 'Parks Pond'. The pond was a sizeable one, with clear water, a gravel bottom, and a steep bank. We always took an ice chest with Dad's beer, and sodas for us. We would all bail in while Dad sipped on his can of beer. He was always the last one in. One memorable occasion stands out in my mind. We had all gone into the pond and were cooling off, laughing, splashing water on each other. Dad gulped down the last swallow of his beer. Then he ran down the bank toward us. Leaping in the air with a "YEEEHAW", as he jumped feet first into the water. As soon as his feet hit the bottom, he emerged with a loud "OOOOUUUUCH", hobbling back up the steep bank on one foot. The other was bleeding profusely. Someone had tossed a broken beer bottle into the water! Dad wrapped a handkerchief around the bleeding foot, which needed stitches. Then he yelled down to us.

"You kids, go ahead and swim for a while. I'll be ok."

The handkerchief was already soaked in blood. We did not remain in the water much longer. Dad didn't have an extra handkerchief! When we arrived home, Mom doctored his foot the best she could, placing on antibiotic ointment, and bandaging it. He was not about to have any stitches. He went to the coal mine the next day with a bandaged foot.

We all enjoyed many happy, fun-filled fishing trips with Mom and Dad as well. There were some occasions when dad would arrive at the fishing spot some miles from home. After arriving there, something would be left behind. Sometimes the fishing poles, sometimes the bucket of minnows. The iced-down beer was always placed into the truck first! I've been on more than one trip with him when this occurred.

"Oh, hell! I left the damn minnows at home! Oh, well, let's have a cold beer. Then we'll go get them."

On these trips, Mom displayed more patience than Dad. She always preferred using a long cane pole which would allow her to toss her line far out into the water. Then she would sit in the shade nearby, her straw hat covering her head. She could sit like this for hours, even if her cork never bobbled. Dad, on the other hand, was not as patient. If a cork never moved after a while, he was ready to find another nearby spot. Mom usually wanted one of us nearby, just in case a large bass should take her minnow. Sometimes she and I would get distracted, talking about various things. Suddenly, she would scream out.

"Oh, Bill! The pole's going out in the water! Go get it!"

There were a number of times when I waded into the water to retrieve her pole. At times, there may be a large fish on the line. At other times, it would be tangled in brush. Sometimes she would be skunked, and I would have to rebait her hook.

If Dad was lucky, he was happy; if not he may become infuriated. One such trip stands out in my mind. Everyone was catching nice fish that day, crappie, bass, even catfish. Dad, however, was not having a good day. He was catching the rough fish......carp, drum, buffalo, even a turtle or two. An angry shout came from down shore a ways.

"I'll be damn! It's another damn carp. Hell, I'm quitting!"

He retrieved the pole from the water, and tossed it onto the rocks, breaking it in two. We were all too afraid to laugh. After a beer or two to quiet his nerves, he did resume fishing again. He still didn't catch any thing worth keeping.

Mom always enjoyed the fishing trips, but the other activities were left to Dad. When we were fortunate enough to have a good snow in the winter time, Dad always joined us for the snow ball fights. He ran around the yard, chasing us and throwing snow balls at us. Because of his pitching abilities, he was usually pretty accurate. I distinctly recall one of these events when other neighborhood kids joined in the fun. One friend, George Finamore, was in brother Sonny's class at school. He came down to join in the fun. We were having quite a time, sliding around, hitting one another with the snow balls. Suddenly someone blurted out.

"Where's George? Has anybody seen George?"

(The snowball crew. From left, brother Sonny, Billy Jeff Miller, Bill Crone, Raymond Willcutt, George Finamore.)

After a short search, we discovered him face-down in the snow. Everyone became frightened. Dad hurried over to him, and shook him by the shoulders.

"George! George! Are you ok? What happened?"

George moaned in pain. "I slipped and fell. I think I hurt my back."

Dad lifted him and escorted him to the house, placing him near the coal stove in the dining room where he could warm himself.

Mom brought him a hot cup of coffee, which he sipped with delight.

"I think I feel better now. I better go on back home now to rest."

George was not severely injured, and was soon back to his old self again.

Billy Jeff Miller was a friend and a neighbor. He was very tall, even in his youth. Bill Crone was dating Marilyn at the time. Raymond Willcutt, shown earlier, later married sister Phyllis. George was a good friend of Sonny and the family.

Winter time also brought about another memorable occasion. Following a good snow, in the evening we would gather east of the home, at a location we called "Charlie Thomas' Hill". Charlie lived just below the hill north of our home. He was one of our black neighbors, and was quite friendly to everyone. At the top of the hill, Dad would always build a fire to warm us. Then everyone would sled down 'Charlie Thomas' Hill'. Some were fortunate enough to have sleds. Others improvised by using garbage can lids, cardboard boxes, or whatever was brought along. When we became cold, we warmed ourselves near the fire Dad had built. Mom never accompanied us on these adventures, but she always had hot coffee and chocolate for us to share when we returned to the house.

Due to the generation Dad grew up in, he never really approved of Negros. This was also something he probably acquired from his father, and grandparents. To him they were "N-----s". You can fill in the blanks! However, there was something quite peculiar about Dad concerning the Blacks that lived in our neighborhood. They were treated like family! Charlie Thomas, mentioned above, would be given fresh vegetables from the garden, choc beer, or anything else Dad could provide. Another black gentleman, John Hanks, lived in a shack in a field south of our home. John Hanks was a very simple man. The grocers in Krebs were aware of this, and they provided him with various items, such as aged bread, outdated lunch meats and the like. He had no running water. Consequently, he would appear at our door from time to time. Mom would go to the door. There stood John Hanks, bucket in hand.

"Now, I don't mean no harm, Miss Scarpett. I just wants to get some water."

Mom always obliged him. "Take your bucket, John. Get as much water as you need."

"Thank yee, Miss Scarpett." He filled the bucket and carried it back to his shack in the field.

Me, my brother Sonny, and George Finamore, would sometimes pay John Hanks a visit. He invited us into his small one-room shack. Grocers always provided him with cans of his favorite food……sardines. He handed George a can opener and a can of sardines.

"Here, George. Open me a can of these sardeens."

George would oblige him, opening the can, and setting it on the table for him. John grabbed a fork, and soon the juicy sardines were gone.

I was a small boy, around 8 years old. Something in the room caught my eye. His old iron bed was sitting up high, resting on a stack of bricks. I had to ask.

"John, why is your bed so high?"

He grinned at me, showing huge white teeth. "That's so the devil won't get me, lil' buddy." He laughed hysterically.

We all joined in the laughter.

John often went around the neighborhood, performing odd jobs for people, to get a little cash. I recall his deadly fear of snakes. One day he was cutting some weeds for a neighbor, Annie Beaver. The weeds were located near a small pond on her property. He was wielding the sickle, swinging it back and forth, the weeds flying in the breeze. Suddenly he stopped, jumping back wide-eyed with fear.

"Snake! Snake!" He shouted. He chopped furiously at the ground with the sickle. Soon a small harmless Garder snake lay in several bloody pieces on the ground. John could not be persuaded to finish the weeding job that day.

Some years later, as I recall, John Hanks was found deceased in his little shack. The story circulated around eleven-and-a-half that he had died from poisoning, a food poisoning brought on by consuming some spoiled lunch meat. I don't know if this was true or not, but I do know that John did not have the luxury of a refrigerator.

MOM AND DAD

There was another Black gentleman who we knew as 'Mr. Homer'. He lived near John Hanks's old shack. Mr. Homer, however, had a nicer, larger home which faced the street. He was a rather small man with a pleasant disposition. I had a tree house near his property, and I would often climb up and have a look around. He had a sizeable corn patch near the tree house. One day as I climbed up, I saw Mr. Homer using a hoe to cultivate his corn crop. As he saw me climbing up, he jokingly raised the hoe and aimed at me, as though firing a rifle. Then he chuckled out loud.

He would sometimes visit our home and Dad would pour him a cold glass of choc beer. Mr. Homer savored Dad's special recipe. He would take a big gulp.

"Boy! Dat' sho' am good beer, Chestuh."

Dad only smiled back, filling his glass again.

Another Black gentleman, mentioned earlier, who lived in our neighborhood was John Chapman. Dad treated him with dignity and respect, as the others in the area. John Chapman could always be seen carrying a toe sack over his shoulder. In here he gathered anything which might bring a nickel, pop bottles, scraps of iron or copper, or anything salvageable. Like John Hanks, he lived in a small one-room shack. It was located a short distance north of our home. A trail leading to our fishing creek passed near John Chapman's house. Clutter was visible for a fair distance around his house.

One cold winter night we were all gathered in our old house on the hill. Dad had popped a huge pan of popcorn, one of his favorites. We were listening to the radio, and playing dominoes. Someone got up to go outdoors and use the outhouse. There was a scream.

"Something big is burning down a way from here!"

We all got up and ran outside. There was a glowing flame and smoke just north of our home. We ran as fast as possible to the scene. It was John Chapman's old shack, practically burned to the ground already. There was a younger woman who lived with him by the name of 'Cora'. He always claimed that she was his niece. However, we all had our doubts. When we arrived at the scene, Cora was standing outside, wrapped in an old gown. We did not see John anywhere. We became frightened.

"Cora!" We shouted. "Where is John?"

"He's over in there!" She pointed to the fire.

"You mean he's in the fire?"

"No. He's on the other side."

We all made our way to the west side of the shack. There was John seated in an old nasty chair, clad in long-handle underwear which were practically as black as he.

"You ok, John?" Someone asked.

"Yeah. I's alright. Just don't has no house no moe'." He laughed, seeming all the while unconcerned.

The old house was soon ashes. I never learned where Cora and John spent that night, or the few days following the fire. It was quite cold and the community was concerned with their survival. The neighborhood soon took up a collection and purchased an old shack similar to the one which burned. It was moved onto the same property. Cora seems to have disappeared. Sometime later this shack also burned to the ground. The community did not seem as concerned with John's welfare after this. It was again cold winter time. A few days after the second shack burned, John was found frozen to death in his chicken coop. It seemed such a sad way to end a poor man's life.

Another Black couple who lived just over the hill to the east of our place were Earl and Lovey May Fields. Earl was a quiet and reserved man, having few words to say, but an occasional smile. Lovey May, on the other hand, was always cheerful and happy. In the spring and summer, she would often appear on our hill. She always wore colorful straw hats……red, blue, orange. she had all varieties. If Dad should happen to be in the garden, she would stop and visit.

"Is you workin' hard, Chestuh'?"

Dad wiped the sweat from his brow. "Not too bad, Lovey May. Let me grab you a bag. Get all the vegetables you want."

She took the bag from Dad's hand. "I sho' do thank ye', Chestuh'. Earl, he just love yo' garden vegetables." She filled the bag and made her way back over the hill.

Things were quite different during those days. I'm sure I was the only white boy around who worked for a black woman. I would sometimes show up at Lovey May's house to see if I could earn 50 cents for a movie. Lovey May would show up on the porch, a wide smile across her face.

"Now, Bill! You knows' you don't wanna' work." She laughed.

"I'll do anything, Lovey May. I want to earn some money to go to the movie."

She scratched her head under the straw hat. "Well, now. Let me see." She gazed around her yard. "Can you pull some weeds out' my garden, cut that grass ovuh' by the fence? I pays' you 50 cents."

"Sure!" I replied. I went to work on hands and knees, pulling the weeds from her garden. She provided me with a small sickle to cut the grass near the fence. I tried to do the best job I could, knowing that she would let me do jobs in the future. I pulled the long grass up with my left hand and swung the sickle nearby, cutting the grass close to the roots. Suddenly, there was a sharp pain as I swung the sickle a little too close.

"Ouuchh!" I screamed, looking down at my bloody little finger. The sickle had sliced into my knuckle. I still bear the scar after all these years.

Lovey May appeared on the porch. "Whatsa' mattuh', Bill?"

I held up my bleeding finger.

"Ooooh, my Lord! Let me go in the house and gets you a band aid!"

She hurried outside to bandage my finger. "Now, you goes' on home. You can finish this job latuh'." She handed me the 50 cents.

"But, Lovey May, I'm not done yet."

"No mattuh! Now, you do like I says. Go on home!"

I made my way back up the hill. Later that afternoon I enjoyed a movie at the Okla Theater in McAlester. The 50 cents also provided popcorn and a coke. Hitch-hiking there and back was no problem during those times.

During the late spring and early summer time, there were always black berries growing on or near our hill. Lovey May dearly loved these, but did not like picking them herself. I would go down to her house and she would provide me with a large lard bucket. If I were lucky, she may even give me a dollar for this.

She met me on the porch, handing me the bucket.

"Now, Bill, this gotta' be full, all the way to the top. I gives you a dolluh! But, gotta' be full!"

"Ok, Lovey May."

I made my way to the top of the hill, in the field across from our house. I waded through chiggers and the thorny berry patches. An hour had passed and the bucket was only two-thirds full. I remember what Lovey May had said. I wanted the dollar, not the 50 cents. Finally, I had the bucket filled to the brim, and my pants loaded with chiggers. I hurried down the hill to Lovey May's house. She met me on the porch, inspecting the bucket.

"You sho' do a good job, Bill. You fill dat' bucket plumb to the top! Here be yo' dolluh."

'Wow! A whole dollar'! I thought, as I made my way back up the hill. That would provide two trips to the movie, and the refreshments.

One really comical incident occurred one day when I was doing some chores for Lovey May. When I was finished, she brought me a cold glass of ice water to the porch, and handed me a small paper bag. I looked inside. It was filled with brazil nuts, only I did not know them by that name. Lovey May stood, looking at me with delight. I cracked one open with a small rock near the porch, and placed the tasty nut in my mouth. Then it came.

"Boy! These sure are good 'Nigger toes', Lovey May."

She looked at me with disgust. "Them ain't no Nigguh' toes, Bill! Them's brazil nuts!"

It was the only name I knew of for the tasty nuts. When I arrived home, and related this story to Dad, he laughed hysterically for it seemed 30 minutes.

My godfather, Pug Rich, lived near Lovey May, and he, too, would allow me to do chores for him to earn money. He lived with his mom, Mary, who was known in earlier times as 'Maria Blue'. The name came about because Pug's father was called 'Blue John'. I don't know how he derived that name. My recollection is that he was killed in a coal mining accident. At any rate, Pug would allow me to cut grass, or pull weeds, or just about any other chore he could find. He was always very generous to his godson. One day he had a two-dollar job. I soon found out why. In the peak of the roof of his storage building there was a large nest of red wasps. Unfortunately, in those times, there were no cans of wasp spray which would reach 20 feet! Pug had a plan. He had placed the ladder beneath the nest. He stood by the ladder with a rolled-up newspaper and a match.

"Now! I want you to climb up the ladder a way. I'm going to light the end of this paper and hand it to you. You hurry up the ladder and burn the wasp nest."

It sounded like a good plan to me. Only, soon I found out it wasn't. Pug handed me the lit newspaper. I hurried up to the nest and stuck the burning newspaper onto the nest. A number of wasps fell to the ground. Others swarmed around my head, trying frantically to escape the flames. I hurried back down the ladder as fast as I could, but soon felt some burning in my pants leg. Some of the red wasps had lost their wings, but not the legs. They ascended that ladder directly into my trousers. Pug laughed hysterically as I raced to the door of his storage building my pants half-way down. His mom soon found some ointment for my stinging legs. Pug was still laughing.

"I think that job was worth three dollars, instead of two." He was still laughing when he handed me the dollars.

I went back up to Anderson Hill, but did not feel much like a movie that day.

Mom was always a dear mother to her baby boy, me of course. She always cared tenderly for me, and in her eyes, I could do no wrong, at least most of the time. Whenever I crossed her, however, it became an entirely different story. She could be a strict disciplinarian when the need arose.

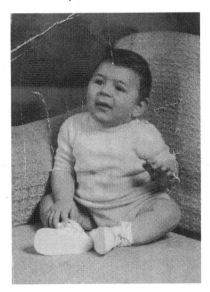

(Wasn't I a darling little baby! Look at all that black hair! And those chubby little legs. Seventy-two years later, not so much so!)

When I was little, Mom usually took up for her baby boy. One incident, in particular, stands out in my mind. During those early times, the winters could be quite cold in the old house. Dad would always load the coal stove in the dining room before he went to bed, but early in the morning when the stove died down, the bedrooms could be quite chilly. Mom tried to keep us warm by covering us with a heavy quilt. Brother Sonny was notorious for pulling the quilt over to his side, leaving me shivering in the cold. Mom soon solved the problem. She searched the house to find the largest safety pin I'd ever seen. She took the pin and pushed it down into the quilt, the sheet, and the mattress cover on my side of the bed. Then she snapped it in place. I was snug all night long! I don't know if sonny ever caught on!

As I approached my teen-age years, I soon learned that Mom also would not take any crap. One day I was spouting off to her pretty badly. I can't recall what I was arguing about, but nonetheless, I was being pretty disrespectful. Without saying a word, Mom reached back and gave me a sharp slap across the cheek. I leaned back, trying to avoid much of the impact. When I did this, she struck my nose, which began to bleed. When this happened, I thought I had it over on her.

"Mom! Look what you did! You made my nose bleed!"

She looked me straight in the eyes.

"That's nothing! Just wait until your Daddy gets home!"

She turned her back on me and walked away. From that time on, I don't recall smarting off to my Mom.

Our Mom was a hard-working woman with a large family to tend to. There was never a time when three meals a day were not on our table, even when she felt her worst. In addition to this, there was cleaning to do, laundry, and canning vegetables from the garden. Laundry was done in what was called "the big shanty". Water had to be hauled from the outdoor faucet. A number of buckets had to be transported there. The old washing machine was one with the wringers attached. Clothes would be washed and then placed in the rollers to be wrung out. They were later placed on the clothes line for drying. The dirty clothes were scrubbed on a wash board, washed, rinsed, and then placed

MOM AND DAD

on the line for drying. In her later years, Mom still bore the scars on her wrists from this hand washing on the scrub board. Luckily, these old-style washing machines were equipped with a release just in case someone should get their hands a little too close while placing the clothes between the rollers. Sonny learned this one day when both arms were engaged between the rollers all the way to his elbows. Mom managed to release the rollers and remove his bruised arms. I don't believe he went near that machine again!

(Sonny in his young teenage years. Notice all the wavy black hair. He liked this hair style. When Dad cut his hair, he teased him about making a spillway in back just in case it rained.)

Growing up, Sonny was always more of a scrapper than I. He would sometimes get into fights, while I usually talked my way out of them. Maybe I was more of a chicken. A time or two, Dad even had to bail him out of jail! And, Sonny was never very big!

He just didn't take any crap. And now that he is 75 years old, he's even more so.

Shortly after Grandpa John passed in 1962, Mom, Dad, Sonny and I moved to Grandma's house for a time to keep her company. Mom was worried about her being alone, and grieving herself to death. Sonny and I shared the old bedroom where Great Grandma Grace slept. Sonny was around 21 years old at this time. The old bedroom had a door which led to a porch on the east side. Sonny would often stay out late drinking with his friends. He had a weak stomach. How many times Sonny would hurry from that bed and dash out onto the porch, heaving violently and loudly. I had to cover my ears, lest I too became nauseated.

One early Saturday morning Sonny dashed into the bedroom. I was already in bed, but there was enough light that I noticed a piece of his bottom lip had a deep gouge. He was snorting and swearing under his breath. Then he ripped off his nasty white t shirt and tossed it under the bed. He headed for the bathroom to clean up. I pretended to be asleep. Of course, the next morning Mom noticed the piece of his lip missing, and the bruises. When she discovered that he was fighting over a girl, she became furious. Dad only laughed.

"Well, I hope you got the best of him."

Mom protested. "Chester!"

"Well, hell, if you're going to fight, you want to win!"

Mom hurried back in the house with a groan of disgust.

Sonny explained. "Well, Dad. He was flirting with my girlfriend and I got mad. He swung at me, and I leaned back, but his thumbnail caught my lip. Then I clobbered him."

Dad did not protest too much, but he warned him about having to bail him out of jail.

As I reentered the house, Mom was still furious, angry at her son, and Dad. Should I tell her about the shirt or not? Oh, well, she would find it anyway.

"Mom, if you look under our bed, I think you'll find something."

She took the old dust broom, pushing it under the bed. Out came the bloody, dirty shirt. Then she really became furious, and I left the house with my fishing pole. I never learned who got the worst of that situation, Dad or Sonny. I do believe she made him buy himself a couple of new t shirts.

Fresh out of high school, Sonny and I played baseball together. We belonged to a thing called "The Little Dixie League". There were a number of teams from the area who belonged to the league. Sonny, being left-handed, always played first base. I, on the other hand, was usually the catcher. Having had polio, I was not fast on my feet. Catching was a position which did not require a lot of running, just some tough hands, coupled with a lot of guts. I was sometimes run over at the plate by a runner trying to score from third base. Seems the runner was always arriving at the plate at the same time as the ball. There was always a collision. Sometimes I could hold onto the ball,

MOM AND DAD

sometimes not. One big player was notorious for running me over. He took advantage of my small size. During one game I got the opportunity to get even. He was lumbering toward me from third base. Fortunately, the throw got to me early. As he came charging in head-first, I stepped back and tagged him out. He hit the ground with a 'thud'. When he arose, his forearm was bent up in the middle. He walked away groaning in pain. He never ran over me again. Neither did I ever see him in another game!

(Sonny in his Army Uniform. He entered into six-months active duty right out of high school, and as I recall, was stationed at Fort Chaffee in Arkansas. Luckily, he never saw any action, for this was during the time of the Viet-Nam War.)

In playing in these baseball games, Sonny's temperament was unchanged. He would argue with the umps regarding balls and strikes. He would argue concerning calls at first base. Sometimes his language was a little abusive to the ears, causing him to get ejected from the game.

Mom and Dad were usually at these games, for they both loved the game. Dad would stand behind the screen when we batted. If we swung at a high or low pitch, or one outside the strike zone, he would protest.

"What the hell are you swinging at? You couldn't reach that with a ten-foot pole!"

Mom was often embarrassed, but she usually kept her cool, and tried to encourage us in a gentler manner.

Dad loved the game, and was always outside warming us up before the game, after we had our Sunday dinner, of course. He always came to the ball games with an ice chest filled with cold choc and sodas for Mom and other family members. The same applied to any picnics we went on, or fishing trips. Refreshments were always provided, including plenty of drinks, chips, sandwiches, even candy for small grandkids. Even the deer camps Dad went on were provided with all the refreshments needed. It did not matter how many men were there, or how many days the deer camp lasted. Dad was generous.

When brother Sonny left home for his six-months active duty, there was a popular song circulating at the time. Each time it came on the radio, Mom began to cry. Some of the words of the song went like this: "Good-by, Jimmy, good-by. Good-by, Jimmy, good-by. I'll see you again, but I don't know when. Good-by, Jimmy, good-by."

It was easy to see how these words touched the heart of a devoted Mother.

While growing up on Anderson Hill, we all soon learned of Mom's fear of the Spring time storms. At the slightest sound of

MOM AND DAD

thunder and lightning, Mom was ready to head for the storm cellar. Sometimes it was warranted; at other times, not so much so. On one occasion, it was definitely time to head for the storm cellar. It was during a May evening in the late 1950's. Phyllis was preparing to graduate high school, I believe that very evening. We were all seated at the kitchen table, having supper. Suddenly an ominous cloud appeared in the southwest. It was a greenish-black wall cloud. Dad headed for his perch on the rock bench outside the kitchen. The cloud began to approach rapidly. He screamed back at us.

"Get in the cellar, NOW!!!"

Phyllis was screaming all the way to the cellar door! We hurried inside, huddling together, and staring out the open cellar door. The threatening cloud was approaching rapidly. Dad raced toward the open door.

"Grab onto something stout! This damn thing will suck you right out of here!"

Phyllis was screaming uncontrollably. I looked out the open door as Dad prepared to close it. There was a radio station to the west of us, about a quarter mile away. The middle tower was lifted into the air in a rotating motion and tossed to the ground. There was a loud roar as Dad closed the door, holding onto it tightly. Would our house be gone? Would we be gone? Suddenly there was a deafening silence. We emerged from the cellar, and looked to the northeast. The tornado missed us. As we looked, we saw a number of small funnels descending and ascending from the cloud. Luckily, we were unharmed. Wilburton, to the east of us was not so lucky. It struck the downtown district, destroying a church, and other buildings, and killing around a dozen people. After this, Mom had us in the cellar whenever a cloud came up!

When we were kids growing up in eleven-and-a-half, occasionally we would receive a good snowfall which stayed on the ground for several days. We enjoyed these times, playing in the snow. Sometimes if the ice were thick enough, we would skate on an ice-covered pond belonging to Anna and Charlie Beaver. It was located just over the hill to the east of our home. Anna was a sister to Pug Rich. From there sometimes we would skate up and down the road on the street near Mr. Johnson's home. You recall, he is the one who had the run-in with Grandpa John mentioned earlier. One memorable occasion stands out in my mind. We were all skating up and down that road one evening, having a delightful time, being rather noisy, as kids often do. Suddenly, Mr. Sid Johnson appeared on his porch.

"Hey, you kids! You get out of here! You're making too much noise! My wife needs to rest. If you don't leave, I'll get a gun after you!"

We ran as fast as possible, slipping and sliding, all the way back to Anderson Hill. We hurried into the house, screaming in fear. Dad was at the kitchen table, shaving. He almost sliced his face with all the commotion. "What the hell's going on?"

"Dad! Mr. Johnson said he's going to shoot us if we skate on the street in front of his house!" We all screamed simultaneously.

"Well, we'll see about that!"

Dad threw his razor down on the table, and wiped his face with a towel.

"You kids follow me!"

We practically hung onto Dad's shirt tail, as he dashed over the hill. When we arrived at Mr. Johnson's gate, Dad yelled at him.

"Sid Johnson! You old son-of-a-bitch! You come out here right now!"

The door screeched open, and Mr. Johnson's head appeared.

"What do you want?"

"What's this I hear about you threatening my kids? Come on out here, and let's talk about this."

Mr. Johnson cautiously made his way to the gate. "Your kids are making a lot of noise, Mr. Anderson. My wife can't rest. I told them to play on another street."

"Well, that's not the story I got! I was told that you threatened to shoot them. Is that right?"

"I did tell them that I'd get a gun." He admitted sheepishly.

"Well, you go get that gun, and I'll make you eat the damn thing!"

Mr. Johnson reached into his overalls pocket, retrieving a pocket knife. He waved it at Dad.

"Well, you just step out here, and I'll make you eat that damn thing too! I'll turn your damn nose up where the rain will run in it!"

We all watched in amazement, as Mr. Johnson turned and hurried into the house, locking the door behind him.

Dad turned to us. "Now, you kids play on this street any time you want to. It's a public street. I don't believe Mr. Johnson will bother you again."

He never did.

Dad loved animals, but their place was outdoors, not in the house. We always had a dog or two, but their place was outside. We never bought dog or cat food. They were fed from the table. Mom called our dogs "pot-lickers". After supper, they would clean out the pots. Cats similarly, were fed outdoors with whatever scraps were left over. I recall a large gray cat we had named "Elvis". In the winter time he was allowed to come in and eat Then he would warm himself near the coal stove. When that was finished, Dad promptly placed him outdoors. We also had a gray dog named "Snippy". He would greet us each morning when we arose to get ready for school. When we went out the door, he always lifted his paw to give us a hand-shake. He was deathly afraid of storms. At the slightest sound of thunder and flashing of lightning, he immediately ran and hid himself under the old wash pot where Dad brewed his choc. Ashes did not bother him. He curled up inside with his head facing the opening. As soon as the storm passed, he emerged covered with black ash.

A peculiar incident occurred one time involving Snippy. Dad always enjoyed hunting, rabbits, squirrels, deer, whatever. He returned from a squirrel hunt one day with a number of squirrels.

(Dad standing near the clothes line in 1958. This was one of his favorite attires in the summer month, overalls and no shirt. He was 43 years old. I don't believe he did the washing though!)

In the process of cleaning the squirrels, Snippy and other dogs were usually around to eat any scraps. A few days after this cleaning process, we noticed Snippy straining to have a bowel movement, but nothing would come out. He howled in pain. Finally, one day, we noticed something protruding from his rectum as he strained to defecate to no avail. Upon closer inspection, we observed a bit of fur sticking out. Dad tried to pull it with his hands to no avail. Snippy growled and snapped at him.

Finally, our neighbor, Mike Pulchny, was summoned. He had in his hands a pair of pliers. This was going to be a difficult procedure. It was going to take more than one person.

"OK, Chester. I'll hold his head. You take that pliers and pull that piece of hide out!"

Dad gritted his teeth, and pulled with all his strength. Snippy howled in pain. Soon a large segment of squirrel hide popped out along with a large amount of blood and fecal material. It seemed Snippy must have crapped for a full hour, but he was greatly relieved. I don't think he attended the squirrel cleanings after that!

Dad was quite a hunter and fisherman. He would often bring home rabbits and squirrels, large fish, and even turtles. He preferred the soft-shell turtles. He cleaned them, and sometimes made turtle soup from them. I was always amazed at the various colored meats in these turtles, ranging from almost black to pure white. I don't believe that Marilyn or Phyllis ever tasted this delicacy, but I was more of a dare-devil. To me, it was quite tasty. Dad would always provide us with the best of the squirrels or rabbits, usually the hind quarters, and maybe the front legs. He would even cook the heads of the squirrels, and remove the brain, which he regarded as a delicacy. Dad often hunted rabbits in the Kinta, Oklahoma area, which provided some quite large swamp rabbits. Sonny was often along on these trips. I preferred the fishing trips, and never took much delight in hunting. I do recall one squirrel hunting trip I went on with Dad. We had to get up early, around 5 in the morning, another reason I did not like squirrel hunting. Dad went ahead of me, quiet as a mouse,

MOM AND DAD

so as not to scare the squirrels. On the other hand, as I trekked through the brush, I cracked limbs and brush noisily. Dad turned to me.

"I'm not ever bringing you again! You make too damn much noise!"

I never would have admitted it, but I was almost glad.

(Here I stand next to a friend, Bill Barry. He was Pug's nephew, who visited each summer from Pensacola, Florida. We always had a great time for a week or so until he had to return home. I am 13, Bill 15.)

Bill Barry grew up and became a Methodist minister. I am a Catholic Deacon, almost 20 years now. Who would have ever thought? I guess Mom prayed for me a lot!

As I look back on my life, I'm lucky to be here. I'm sure that I had a very busy guardian angel, and a Mom who prayed continually for me, as well as Dad and her other children.

MOM AND DAD

I was around 11 years old one day, when I was making my way to St. Joseph School ground to play baseball with other boys. I was riding my bike, my glove attached to the handle bars. I was riding up 'Rough Road', today called "Blake Avenue". Coming toward me were two boys, galloping on their horses. I knew them, Cecil Farley and Ronnie Vicars. I thought in my mind 'Well, I'll just ride my bike, staying in the middle of the road. They would gallop toward me on either side.' The last thing I recall was a horse leaping over my head. I awoke in the ditch with my wrecked bicycle on top of me. Cecil and Ronnie were too scared to stop. They thought they killed me. When I was coming around, a man was shaking my shoulders.

"Billy! Billy! Are you alright?"

It was a man I knew, Wade Beams. He was on his way to Thresa Dominic's house to have some choc beer.

"Those damn boys didn't even stop, Billy! Oh, my gosh! There's blood running from your head! I'm going to take you to your house."

He loaded me and the wrecked bike into his car, a 1955 Chevrolet. Then he dropped me and the bike off at our yard.

"Are you sure you're ok, Billy? I can help you into the house."

"I think I'm alright, Mr. Beams." I cried, as I hurried into the kitchen. I entered the kitchen sobbing loudly. Dad was at the kitchen table with his pan of soapy water, shaving. He heard the commotion.

"Now, what the hell has happened?" He asked, disgustedly, as he turned to have a look at me. Then he saw the blood running down the side of my head. He threw the razor down.

"Oh, my God! What happened?"

Mom soon emerged with a wet wash cloth, and started cleaning the blood away. There was a sizeable gash in the top of my head.

Through sobs, I was soon able to relate what had happened. Mom was quite concerned.

"Chester, that's a deep cut, and there are bruises on him. We better take him to the hospital."

Dad agreed, and we were soon loaded into the car. At the hospital, I received a number of stitches and a tetanus shot. When my shirt was removed, there was a large mark resembling a hoof scrape on my left chest. The horse could not quite clear me. Dad spoke up.

"Damn, boy! You're lucky you weren't killed!"

The incident did keep me out of school for a couple of days, so that Mom could keep her eye on me. I never quite felt the same about horses since that time. I developed a fear of being near them.

A couple of years later another bad mishap occurred. Brother Sonny had just gotten his driver's license. I was 13 years old at the time. Sister Phyllis was working at the Kress store in

McAlester. One evening Sonny and I were assigned to go pick her up from work. Sonny was allowed to drive Dad's 1952 blue Chevrolet. We arrived at the store and picked up Phyllis without incident. On our return, we were not so lucky. Sonny was driving down 69 Highway, only two lanes at that time. We were all in the front seat, Phyllis in the middle, and me near the passenger door. As we approached the exit on Electric Avenue, Sonny placed his arm out the window, indicating a right turn. I don't recall if the car was equipped with turn signals at this time or not. I do know that he gave the signal. As we were turning right, I glanced up and there was the front of a bus heading straight for me! The bus struck us broadside and carried us quite a distance down the highway. No seatbelts at that time! Luckily, the bumper of the bus jammed into the door frame of the car. Otherwise, we would have been rolled over. Phyllis' scream could be heard for miles. We totaled Dad's car, but no one received a scratch. I attribute this again to Mom's persistence in prayer. Oddly enough, the bus was filled with soldiers. They began to emerge to see what had happened. A couple sitting in the back were astonished.

"We didn't know there was an accident. We thought we only stopped for a red light."

Some were making eyes at Phyllis. Of course, they all wanted to console her. She was shaking and crying uncontrollably. As a matter of fact, we were all quite scared.

Dad soon learned of the mishap, and arrived at the scene, clad in his overalls, holding a garden hoe in his hand.

"Now, how the hell did this happen?"

He seemed unconcerned for us, which I'm sure was not the case. When Mom got wind of his reaction, however, she was not too pleased. Dad soon offered his love and concern for us. And he soon learned that the accident was the bus driver's fault. He also soon realized that it was miraculous that no one was injured.

(Above, Phyllis stands in front of the old blue Chevrolet, August of 1958. She was 19 years old. It's easy to see the soldiers' attraction.)

As a small boy growing up in Krebs, I was constantly looking for a way to earn a dollar. The people in the neighborhood were always generous. Not only were there Pug and Lovey May, but also, others. Directly across the street from Pug's house was a lady named Stella Dominic. Her Dad was known as 'Blind Pete'. He had lost his sight in a coal mining accident. She was quite generous, paying me three dollars for my mowing job. Sometimes she would not be at home, and 'Blind Pete' would pay me for the job. I was always amazed as he would count out the three dollars and hand them to me. How did he know the difference between a one dollar bill and a five? Perhaps no one had fives in those days! Or, maybe Stella had provided him with the money before she left home. Anyway, the payment was always correct.

There was something else which amazed me about Pete. Although blind, he could weed his garden, make choc beer and wine, and do other chores. I often watched him as he counted out the steps from his porch to the cellar. There were a certain number of steps until he reached the first step descending into the cellar. He never missed. One day I showed up to cut the grass. He was outside near the cellar.

"Pete! I'm here to cut the grass."

"Beely! Sure, you come. I pay you."

Pete seemed a little upset that day.

"Is something wrong, Pete?"

"Dirty som-un-a-bitch! Someone come, stealuh' my wine!"

"You're kidding!"

"No kid! He's all gone. I havea'make new."

I felt sorry for 'Blind Pete', that someone would take advantage of him.

Another lady's lawn I mowed during those times was that of Caroline Naush. She was a widow woman who lived across the ball park from our home. She had been widowed for years and always dressed in black. She always had a number of goats grazing in her yard. One morning before I started off for her house to mow, Mom caught my arm.

"I want you to go by the post office first and mail these letters. Pick up the mail and bring it home."

"OK, Mom." I pecked her on the cheek, and hurried out the door. This was a three-dollar job, and Caroline would usually feed me, too. Always a delicious bowl of her famous spaghetti and meat sauce. I rushed to the post office, mailed the letters, and retrieved our mail. I placed the mail on Caroline's porch before I began the mowing job. When finished, she paid me, and fed me as usual. When I went to the porch, I couldn't believe my eyes. Shredded mail was scattered all over the place. The goats had gotten their fill of our mail. It looked like it had gone through a shredder. I was afraid to go home. I felt like I, too, would be placed in a shredder. Mom understood, though. It was probably all bills anyway. They would be sent again.

During the time we grew up on Anderson Hill, there was no bathroom in the house. Taking a bath involved filling a wash tub with warm water which was placed in the kitchen. After bathing was finished, the tub was carried outside and emptied. The toilet, common in those early times, was some distance north of the house. Almost everyone in our neighborhood had an out-house. When it became too full, Dad had a nasty job. A wheel barrow was placed behind the out-house, and with a shovel Dad removed all the sewage and buried it in the garden in a deep pit. He placed lime in the newly excavated outhouse pit, and as it began to fill, he would occasionally place lime on top, cutting down the smell, and the flies.

One winter night I was afflicted with diarrhea. It was late at night, but I was afraid to wake anyone. I grabbed a flashlight and hurried to the toilet. As I sat there relieving myself, I heard snorting, and rooting near the outhouse. Charlie Thomas raised hogs, and one of them escaped. I almost froze to death! I must have sat there for more than an hour, listening until the snorting had stopped. I was shivering. I slowly creaked the door open, listening. I heard nothing. Then I ran as fast as possible back to the house. I ran inside. Mom was standing near the coal stove.

"My God, son! What took you so long? I was about to come down to see if you were alright."

I backed my butt up near the warm stove. "One of Charlie Thomas's hogs got loose, and he was snorting by the toilet. I was afraid to come out."

"Well, you finish warming yourself. Then get in bed. You have school tomorrow."

She never asked me whether the diarrhea was over!

MOM AND DAD

Billy Jeff Miller, mentioned earlier, was a good friend of mine and our family. He was very tall for his young age. He derived the nickname, "Goat". Here's how. For some reason, on his way home from school each day, he would bash his head against a stop sign nearby. Everyone began to call him "hard head", which eventually led to "Billy Goat", or simply "goat".

(Above Phyllis stands next to Billy Jeff. His height is pretty evident. Phyllis was 19. Billy Jeff was 16. This, again, is on the west side of the old home place, May of 1959)

Billy Jeff would often appear at our old home on the hill. Sometimes he would challenge all of us neighborhood kids to a game of football, us against him. Our combined efforts could not tackle him! He would drag us along to the end zone.

He also had a voracious appetite. He would sometimes appear at our house, holding a full pumpkin pie and a spoon. The entire pie would be consumed in a matter of minutes. We were never offered a bite. One Sunday he appeared just as we were preparing to have our dinner. Mom had fixed a large pan of her famous meatballs and spaghetti. Guests were served first, so Billy Jeff dug in. We watched as he raked practically all the meat balls onto his plate.

"I'm sorry, Mrs. Anderson. I didn't mean to get all the meatballs. They were just on top."

"It's ok, Billy Jeff. There's plenty."

There was plenty of spaghetti, alright. The rest of us had to share a couple of meat balls.

Christmas Eves at our home on the hill were always a delightful time. Mom always fixed her delicacy of cod fish and spaghetti, a tradition brought from Italy. It was not a favorite of we kids, but we pretended to love it anyway. No one wanted to hurt Mom's feelings. Luckily, some of the cod fish was also baked, which was a little more tolerable. Other foods were also available. Dad would always go out with us to pick a cedar tree to cut down, bring home, and decorate. We never failed to receive at least one gift each, which Dad struggled to provide on a coal miner's pay. At the Carbon Mine where he worked, we also received a huge Christmas stocking filled with goodies. One Christmas my big wish was to get a bicycle. There under the tree was a green bicycle, with solid rubber tires. Green was Dad's favorite color.

It seemed that everyone in eleven-and-a-half was at our house on Christmas Eve. The wine and choc were flowing freely. Dad never allowed glasses to be empty. Sometimes visitors would protest.

"I've had enough, Chester!"

Dad only smiled, as he spread the fingers covering the glass, and poured it full again. When people left, they were pretty tipsy. Chick Sellers would usually be there also. He, too, would leave a little staggery. His usual Christmas gift to our family was a large box of chocolate-covered cherries. When he left the house, he would consistently back out of the yard straight into the ditch. Since he was a clutch-rider, the old car did not have a lot of pull. He would reenter the house.

"Son of a bugger! I backed into the ditch again!"

We would all go outside and help push Chick's old car out of the ditch. The roar of the engine could be heard as he rode the clutch all the way back to his house.

One Christmas Eve, Billy Jeff was at the house. He was around 15 years old. Each time someone left, he would polish off what little wine or choc was left in their glass. After some hours, we began to miss him. The search began. We finally located him in the little club house we had built below the hill from the big shanty. This little house was equipped with electricity, a radio, and two bunk beds. Dad would even sleep in here occasionally when he and Mom had a difference of opinion. Billy Jeff was stretched out on the bottom bunk. He was equipped with false teeth, uppers and lowers, which were missing. When he awakened, he reached for his mouth.

"Oh, no!"

"What's the matter, Billy Jeff?" Someone asked.

"I must have puked my teeth out! I have to find them! Mom'll kill me!"

We didn't want to tell him, but his Mom was probably going to kill him when she smelled his breath. With flash light, we searched the yard, and soon he located his teeth in a pile of smelly vomit. After washing his teeth off under the outdoor faucet, he staggered into the kitchen where we gave him strong coffee. Soon there was a knock at the kitchen door. It was his older brother Ludwell. He took one look at his younger brother, the blood-shot eyes, the horrible breath, and the wobbly head. He grabbed him by the arm.

"OK, buddy! Let's go home where you can face Mom."

Billy Jeff was almost in tears as they made their way back over the hill. I didn't see him for a few days, neither did I see him drink choc or wine again.

The fourth of July was also a holiday which our family always enjoyed. There were always picnics and fireworks. One memorable fourth went like this. I was probably 8 or 9 years old. Lake Eufaula was not in the making yet. We were going to picnic at Robbers Cave State Park in Wilburton. Dad was getting ready, the fishing poles, bait, picnic food, the ice chest, and of course the choc beer. As he prepared to ice down the choc beer and soda, suddenly there was a loud crash and the rumbling of cans and trash next to us. We rushed over to the Pulchny's. Erma Pulchny's car was resting in the trash dump.

(Marilyn stands near her bedroom door, the 'big shanty' behind her. The storm cellar is located beneath the shanty. February of 1956. She was 19 years old.)

Screams were coming from the car. Her brakes had gone out, and she sailed right over the driveway into the rubble. Dad hurried to the car door.

"Erma, are you alright?"

"Yeah, Chester. I think the brakes went out. Mike's gonna' kill me!"

"Oh, I don't think so. He'll be glad you're ok."

Erma was right. Mike heard the commotion and soon appeared on the scene.

"Now, what the hell happened?" He seemed unconcerned with his wife, only the car.

"I think your brakes went out." Responded Dad. "It's a good thing that Erma wasn't hurt."

"Now, how and the hell am I gonna' get this car out of all this shit?"

Erma was crying all the while, as we helped her out of the car. Meanwhile, Dad hurried over to our house to finish preparing for our outing. He carried the ice chest to the shanty. Soon, we heard a loud "POP". Dad came rushing out of the shanty holding his thumb, which was bleeding profusely.

"What happened, Chester?" Mom asked, as she hurried to him with a wash cloth.

"A damn bottle of choc blew up!"

The thumb was hanging at a strange angle, and the blood was gushing. A sharp piece of glass had severed the leader in his left thumb. Our picnic had to be delayed for a time as he made a trip to the ER for stitches. The doctor who sewed him up was F. T. Bartheld, an old doctor I became acquainted with many years later when I worked as a med tech. He took a look at Dad's thumb.

"How did this happen?"

"I was icing down some pop when one of them blew up." Dad replied, with a half grin."

"Yeah! Pop hell!" The old doctor replied, as he began to sew up the thumb.

About an hour later Dad drove up, and we headed for Robbers Cave, bandaged thumb and all. There was a lot of choc and pop drinking that day, and good eats. Some of us swam in the cool waters of Carlton Lake. We also fished, including Mom and Dad. He could still throw the pole out, because the damage was on the left thumb. Holding the pole with the left hand, however, was a little more difficult and painful. That evening we watched Dad's grand fireworks show before heading back home. It was a fun-filled day, as usual.

As I spoke of earlier, we always had a chicken coop and a number of hens along with a rooster or two. I recall venturing out to the coop on a Saturday night with Dad, flashlight in hand. We would go select a fattened hen for Sunday dinner. Dad would shine the light in their blinking eyes. Then he would locate one which he thought might make a tasty Sunday dinner.

"What do you think, boy? You think this one will feed us?"

"She looks pretty good to me, Dad."

He grabbed the fattened, clucking hen by the neck, and gave a mighty twist. After the dancing and fluttering were over, the hen was brought into the house and placed in a large pot of boiling water. The smell was better at Sunday dinner! The feathers were then plucked out, and the hen was rotated over an open flame on the range to singe off all the hair. Then the smell really picked up! After gutting, the hen was ready for cooking. It always tasted delicious at the Sunday dinner table, along with other things, like vegetables from the garden. If we were fortunate, Billy Jeff would not show up until dinner was finished!

(Above Sonny checks out Marilyn's old 51 Ford. She purchased this car while working at St. Mary's Hospital in McAlester. Sonny was in charge of maintaining it for her. March of 59. He was 19 years old.)

Regarding the chicken coop, I recall a ferocious rooster we had when I was a small boy. He was a large white rooster, with a long comb on his head, and some nasty spurs. It was frightening to go in the hen house to gather eggs, or to feed the chickens. I always waited until Mr. Mean was at the other end of the chicken yard. Then I would rush in to gather the eggs. He would usually see me and greet me at the coop or at the gate, plucking at me with his beak, or digging those dagger spurs into me. Finally, I'd had enough of "Mr. Mean." One day I cautiously went in to gather the eggs. This time I carried a long wooden broom handle. Sure enough, about the time I had gathered the eggs, and was about to leave the coop, he appeared, clucking wildly, and jumping up to stab me with those spurs. I reached back, and with all my strength, I swung the handle at his head. There was a "CRACK", and the old guy went down. He lay motionless. 'Oh, God', I thought. I've killed the rooster. Now I'm going to be dead meat. I looked down at the old white guy. There was a groove on the side of his head from the blow, and blood was dripping down. What could I do? I hurriedly grabbed the old rooster by his feet and took him to the outdoor faucet. I turned the water on and stuck his head in the gushing stream. Suddenly there was movement. He began to shake his head, and cluck weakly. I hadn't killed him, but I believe he thought he was dead. I set him loose, and he staggered around in circles in the yard. Finally, he regained his composure, and headed back through the open gate to the chicken yard. I never told Mom or Dad what happened, but the rooster avoided me from that time on. I don't know if you can teach an old dog new tricks, but you can sure teach an old rooster new ones!

It was rather comical at times, if you wanted to call it that, growing up on Anderson Hill. Dad and Sonny were very similar in their stubbornness and temperament, as well as their opinions on things. Seems they would argue over anything, even from what direction the wind was blowing. I would usually sit back and laugh. They had opinions on everything, and their opinions always differed. There would be heated arguments, even swearing, which usually brought Mom to the forefront.

"Do you two have to use that kind of language?"

It seems that that just infuriated them all the more. Despite their differences, Sonny and Dad had a deep love and respect for one another. They spent many happy days hunting rabbit, squirrel, and deer together. Sonny even built his home directly across the street from Mom and Dad, and always helped them out in their advancing years.

As I related earlier, Dad was not much of a church-goer, for reasons also described earlier in the book. However, one Christmas Eve was quite memorable. He had had a lot of choc beer. As it began to approach mid-night, he expressed the desire to attend Mid-night Mass with us. He went into the bedroom. Several moments went by. Dad was not coming out. He had gone in to put his "Sunday" clothes on. We went into the bedroom and located him. He was near his closet. One leg was in his suit pants, the other out. He was sound asleep on the floor. When we returned from Mass, he was still there. Mom covered him with a blanket, and we all went to bed to await the arrival of Santa.

As described earlier, when I was 11 years old I was afflicted with polio. It was the year 1955, and this disease was striking the area. Many of my acquaintances were affected very severely. I was more fortunate. For about a week, I was experiencing vague symptoms. My limbs were weak. Occasionally one leg would collapse, causing me to fall. I ran a low-grade fever. I just didn't feel right. Finally, I was admitted to St. Mary's Hospital in McAlester. A series of tests were performed on me. All of them came back negative. At that time, there, was no test for Polio diagnosis, or no vaccine. I was given medicines to lower the fever. After about a week, not finding anything wrong, I was dismissed. I returned home, and after two or three weeks, Mom and Dad noticed that I began to drag my left foot, and it turned toward the inside. After examination, locally again, I was sent to a Dr. Dandridge in Muskogee, Oklahoma. He was an orthopedic physician who had seen many cases of polio. Dad described to him what had been going for the past month or so. The heavy-set doctor looked at me.

"Son, I want you to take your trousers off and walk across the floor for me."

I was a bit embarrassed, but I obliged. I walked across the room, and returned to him and Dad.

Dr. Dandridge looked at Dad. "Well, what do you say it's polio?"

Dad gave him a look of surprise. "What?"

"Yeah. I'm quite sure that's what it is, Mr. Anderson. I've seen enough cases lately to make quite an accurate diagnosis by what I see. Your son's pretty lucky. He has been affected only slightly."

"What can we do?" Dad asked.

"Well, first of all, his arch in this left foot has collapsed completely. The muscle holding it up is around 70 to 80% gone. I could do surgery, but I don't recommend it. I could transplant a muscle from the opposite side of the foot for an instep muscle. The problem is it would be hard to gauge how much muscle to transplant. If I put too much, it would turn the foot too much to the outside."

"What are the other options?" Dad queried.

"Well, I'm going to recommend some exercises, and also building up his left shoe. We need to place a rubber arch support inside, and also a steel wedge in the heel and sole of his shoe, to give him about a quarter-inch lift on the inside. I will send you to a local shoe shop where these things are performed. He has also lost some muscle structure in his left toes. This may sound silly, young man, but I want you to get a shoe box and place some marbles inside. Pick them up with your bare toes at least three times a day for at least ten minutes. Then I want you to try to develop the muscle that holds up your instep. Here's what you'll do. Turn that foot inward as far as possible, and hold that position for a few seconds, then relax. Do this over and over for about twenty times. Also, do this exercise for three times a day. This may help to restore at least some part of this muscle. Then I want to see you back in about three months, alright?"

We thanked Dr. Dandridge as we left his office. The left shoe was built up, and the exercises began. The marble picking did help the toe muscles somewhat, but even today they still curl downward. We returned to Dr. Dandridge's office for a couple of follow-up visits. However, I never regained much of my instep muscle. Today, at the age of 72, I consider myself lucky to not have been afflicted so severely. The 'Post-Polio Syndrome' which struck many a few years back did not affect me. Today I wear an ankle brace on the left side, and I construct my own arch wedge for my left shoe, which works really well. I can still get around pretty well, doing the things I love, like gardening, fishing, and searching for Indian relics. About four years ago, I did need a left hip replacement, as the result of polio on that side. The right knee is going south because of favoring that side for all these years. I suppose that will be the next bionic bone replacement. But, thank God. We can go to the bone yard during our times!

During those early times in the 1950's one of the best times people enjoyed was going to the drive-in-movie. We were no exception. It was usually on a Friday or Saturday night. We would load everyone in the old Chevrolet. A neighborhood kid or two might even be placed in the trunk! We all gathered in the car as Dad swallowed down the last gulp of cold choc. He would come to the car, two or three quarts of choc beer wrapped in newspapers under his arm. Kids in the back seat or floor board were covered with blankets, so as not to have to pay a few cents extra for their fee. Mom and Dad payed around 50 cents each for admittance. Then we drove in and found our spot. There were posts on which were mounted out-door speakers with a wire attached. Kids began to emerge from the car and headed for the outdoor concession stand. If we were lucky, Dad might have a few extra nickels and dimes for a refreshment. During intermission, kids were constantly running around the concession stand, the playground at the back, even between the cars. On one of our excursions our friend Billy Jeff was along. We were running between cars, chasing one another, ducking under the wires of the speakers. The speakers were placed inside the car window, which was partially rolled up to support the speaker. Billy Jeff had a hard time ducking under because of his height. Soon there was a loud "CRACK". His neck caught a wire, bursting out someone's side window. The man was not too pleased with what had happened, but after seeing the horrified look on Billy Jeff's face, he let him off easy, only a warning to slow down!

One such trip to the drive-in movie is even more memorable. During the movie, a voice came over the speakers. At the same time, the siren of an ambulance was passing by.

"Pete Pulchny, please come to the concession stand for an urgent message! Pete Pulchny!"

Pete was Mike Pulchny's brother. Mike, our next-door neighbor was working the night shift at the Carbon Coal Mine. Mike had been critically injured in a mining accident. Two cars quickly left the theater……ours and that of Pete Pulchny. Mike was like a brother to Dad. A large rock had fallen on Mike, crushing his pelvis, and breaking other bones. Doctors wondered if he would even survive. There was little hope of him ever walking again. But, Mike was a tough 'Polander', as Dad called him. With artificial bits of bone, and whatever was used to piece him together again, he walked again, and not even with a limp! He never returned to coal mining, but made a good living with scrap iron, and selling his famous choc beer. He even tore down houses for people, keeping lumber and other items of value. Even politicians would savor his choc recipe, including Gene Stipe, a former state senator. Everyone was on Mike's side. During these times, his delicious choc could be had for 50 cents a bottle, or three for a dollar. Try that today!

During these early times, Dad also brewed choc beer. He, too, had a select group of visitors who delighted in his choc. His he sold for 25 cents a quart bottle. With his generous heart, he gave most of it away. The little money he did take in helped to buy a few groceries. Charlie Beaver, Annie's husband, lived just below the hill from us. He was a Native American with a savor for alcoholic beverages. I swear he knew Dad's brewing night by following his nose. We would be up in that old shanty bottling choc when Charlie would appear at the door. Dad always kept a glass near the crock for him. He dipped down into the crock and retrieved Charlie two or three glasses full which he gulped down with delight. Then he bade us farewell and staggered back over the hill toward home.

Dad also brewed delicious home-made wines, and sumptuous home-made root beer for we kids.

To this day, I vividly recall my first day of school at St. Joseph's. My three siblings had gone before, and had placed the fear of God into my heart. In those times, there was no pre-school, or kindergarten. I started right off in the first grade. They told me of the horrors of a "Sister Mary Clare", a very old and cranky nun. They told of how she kept a 'board' on her desk for spankings, and how she would pinch your ear. I was scared to death. Mom got me up that first morning. She plastered my black hair down with 'Wild Root Cream Oil Hair Tonic'.

"Now, don't be afraid, Billy. Your brother and sisters are only teasing you. Sister Mary Clare is not that bad."

The first day or two, she still had to walk me to school, and chase me back when I started to follow her home.

(St. Joseph's Catholic School where I attended through 8th grade. This school was constructed in 1953, when I was 9 years old. The old wooden school behind this one burned earlier. So, I attended this school from 3rd through 8th grades, graduating through these doors in May, 1959.)

Sister Mary Clare was a little frightening, but not as bad as I had been led to believe. I soon learned to get on the good side of her. She was quite old, and looked to be in her 90's, although I'm sure she may have been a bit younger. Every morning before school, we processed to the Church for Mass. Sister Mary Clare would inevitably fall on our return to the school. I walked along side of her to help her up. She had a country style of speaking.

"Now, that's kind of you, that there now, William." She said, as I helped her to her feet.

This became a ritual for me practically every day, helping Sister Mary Clare into the classroom. She did carry a large wooden paddle on her desk. To my eyes, it looked like a carved-down one-by-four, and she did not hesitate to use it when she thought necessary. There was little nonsense in her classroom. I, however, became her pet, soon learning how to be on her good side. She soon handed me the post office key, and allowed me to walk to the post office during study period to retrieve the Sisters' mail. I returned to the class room, handing her the mail.

"Now, that's very kind of you, that there now, Anderson. You come over to the house. I have a treat for you."

She walked with me to the convent, their small house near the school. She retrieved a nice large piece of cake for me, and a glass of juice.

"Now, I have to get back to the class. You finish that up, that there now, and come to the class."

"OK, Sister." I said, through a mouthful of delicious cake.

During these early times, the Benedictine Nuns wore the full habit. All that was visible were their faces and their hands. Even ears were covered by the full habit. During these times, there was no air conditioning in the school, so in warm months, like early fall and late spring, classes were sometimes held on the porch of the convent. All sisters carried a large black rosary which was hung over their black belts. During study periods, Sister Mary Clare would assign us some work, and then she could be heard whispering loudly as she prayed her rosary. If there was any noise, she immediately responded with a loud crack of her paddle on her desk.

"Now, cut out the monkey work back there, that there now, and get to studying!"

The room grew amazingly silent.

Occasionally, we could distract Sister Mary Clare, and get out of studying for a while. Someone once asked her a question.

"Sister, how was it when you were growing up? When you were a little girl? Were things hard? How did you get to school?"

Sister would put down her rosary, and relate to us the difficulties of those times, the poor families, and how she would have to walk for some distance to and from school, despite the weather. Then she picked her rosary back up.

"That's enough, that there now! Get back to work!"

The principal during this time was a nun by the name of Sister Mary Patricia. She was tall, and rather stern. She had a long nose, and some of we students, especially the boys, gave her a nick name......"Eagle Beak". However, we did not call her this when we addressed her. We soon learned that she was deathly afraid of the springtime storms which often struck our area. When clouds came up, she always posted two of the guys at the doors to watch the clouds. This was usually me and my class mate, Nikey Fassino. We soon learned to spot "tornadic activity". As soon as a black cloud appeared on the horizon, we ran to Sister Mary Patricia.

"Boy, that cloud looks really bad, sister! Maybe, you should dismiss the class so they can hurry home to their storm cellars!"

Usually, this worked, and the class would be dismissed a couple of hours early. One time, though, it was not a false alarm. There was a wall cloud approaching rapidly. Most of the class hurried to Tony Bob DeGiacomo's storm cellar, located near the school. Others living nearby hurried home. Luckily, we were missed again.

It seems like it took forever for these early school days to pass by, but finally I graduated 8th grade, and was ready to begin my freshman year at St. John's in McAlester in the fall of 1959. Again, I was always looking for a way to earn a buck. During that summer, I went to work at the newly-opened Giacomo's Italian restaurant on 69 by-pass. The owner was a big, round Italian man by the name of Dom Giacomo. I earned a whopping three dollars a day, washing dishes, cleaning bathrooms, and clearing off tables. There were no fancy automatic dish washers at that time. All dishes, pots and pans, were scrubbed and rinsed by hand.

Dom would sometimes inspect my work. He stood over me staring at the water in the sink.

"Would you take a bath in that nasty water? Put some clean hot water in that damn sink!"

As he walked away, I uttered a little profanity under my breath as I drained the nasty water and refilled the sink.

Dom's brother, Nick, also worked at the restaurant. It was a family-operated business, owned by Dom. Sometimes I witnessed some heated arguments between the two. One in particular was quite frightening. I don't recall what the dispute was about, but Dom was waving a butcher knife in Nick's face.

"I'll cut you with this damn knife, you son-of-a-bitch!"

Nick picked up a huge watermelon in the kitchen. "Yeah, and I'll smash this damn watermelon over your head, too."

'Brotherly love', I thought, as I watched the drama unfold. Finally, the stand-off was over. Nick removed his white apron.

"I'm quitting!" He removed the apron and threw it in the corner.

"Yeah, you go ahead and quit!" Dom snapped back. "You can go back to driving that damn pop truck for $25 a week, like before!"

MOM AND DAD

Nick walked out the door, and stepped over to Tony Town next door, a sort of hardware store that was newly opened. Here he cooled off, and soon returned to work, putting his apron back on, as though nothing had happened. He looked at me.

"He didn't mean all that stuff. He just gets mad some time."

(An inside view of St. Joseph's School, which has now become our parish hall. The middle-class room was located here, where 4th, 5th, and 6th grades were held, the domain of Sister Mary Clare)

Nick went back to work, like nothing ever happened. Both behaved like there had never been a dispute. It was the Italian way.

One other event took place during my work days there, which I shall never forget. It was on a weekend, and the restaurant was filled to capacity. Nick was busy, taking orders, cleaning tables, doing everything he could to keep customers happy. I was doing my dish-washing duties, under the supervision of Dom, when Nick hurried to us.

"Dom, there's a customer out there that I just can't please. This is not right; that's not right, the steak's not cooked right, the prices are too high! I can't take any more of his shit!"

I watched in horror as Dom took off his apron, and tossed it on the floor. He dashed out to the man's table, with a restaurant full of hungry customers. He got right up into the man's face.

"Bull shit, Mr.! You come in this restaurant and sink in carpet up to your ass! And you complain about things not being right, and the prices too damn high. If you don't like our prices, then get your ass out of here, and don't come back!"

There was the sound of gasps, and silverware hitting the table, as Dom retreated back to the kitchen. To my recollection, the man did finish his meal, and pay the tab, but I never saw him there again during my tenure there.

I worked at Giacomo's for most of that summer of 1959. Then, being a kid, I'd had enough. I just didn't show up for work one day. I was out in our yard when Dom drove up in his long Lincoln Continental. He rolled down the window.

"Hey, aren't you coming to work today?"

"No, Mr. Giacomo. I'm tired. Besides, I've got to start back to school pretty soon. I want a week or so to relax."

He gave me a look of disgust and a snarl.

"What the hell! What are you, some kind of Nigger or something?"

That irritated me a bit. I glared in the window at him. "No! Are you?"

There was the sound of tires squealing as the Lincoln headed over the hill.

That fall of 1959 I entered St. John's Catholic School in McAlester as a freshman. It was also headed by the Benedictine Nuns, who were again quite strict. There was little nonsense in their classrooms. If it became a little over-bearing the parish priest was summoned to quiet things down. If one had a girl friend, even in high school, he'd best not be found holding her hand on school property. This brought strict disciplinary measures.

When I became a sophomore, that winter we had something unusual. There was a great snowfall, which remained on the ground for a week or more. Classes, of course, continued as usual. The hour after lunch was a study period, so myself and a few other buddies thought we would take advantage of it. A couple of them lived nearby, so after lunch we headed for 5th street hill, a steep snow-covered hill located near the school. We sledded down that hill, having a grand time, and felt it perfectly alright to miss the study hour. After all, we could make it up later. When it approached time for the first class, we decided it best to head back to the school. We marched right into the class, just like nothing happened. There was utter silence. Sister Judith watched as we removed our coats and hung them in the closet.

(St. Joseph's Catholic Church, where I've attended from my infancy. Here my Grandfather John brought me to 6:30 AM Mass as a boy. The church, constructed in 1903, is one of the oldest, most beautiful churches in the Diocese of Tulsa. Here I've served as deacon at Mass for nearly 20 years now. What a great privilege!)

After hanging our coats, we sat down as usual. Sister Judith spoke up.

"You boys, get up right now, and march yourselves to the library! Sister Mary John will meet you there shortly."

It was then that we knew we were in deep trouble. After a good scolding by the strict Mary John, we were all given a two-week assignment to be performed after school each afternoon. This assignment consisted of writing a 500-word paper on why we would not miss school again. It was hard to make up that many reasons for not missing, covering a two-week period. After that, I don't recall any of us missing again.

During the 1960's, the New York Yankees were practically unbeatable. Every year they were in the World Series and always won. Sister Mary John was an avid Yankees fan. During the world series, she placed a radio on her desk, and assigned us work to do, while she listened to the world series. She would turn the volume down, placing her ear to the radio. Many of us there loved the series, but were pulling for the other team. We would beg her.

"Sister, please! Can you turn the volume up just a little?"

She gave us a strict look, but usually obliged by turning it slightly so we could hear a bit. The sound of her applause could be heard in the classroom when the Yankees scored another run.

I made it through another 4 years with the Benedictine Nuns, graduating in May, 1962, in a class of ten. Grandpa John passed away only about a month before my graduation.

Our Mom always had a sort of premonition character about her, a sense of when something was about to happen. During a cold winter night in 1960, her senses were on high alert. Dad was working the night shift at the Carbon Coal Mine. After he left for work, Mom could not rest. She was up out of bed, pacing the floor. We all questioned her.

"Mom, what's wrong? Can't you sleep?"

"I don't know, kids. Something's not right. Something's wrong. I can feel it."

We all went back to bed, except Mom. But, no one could sleep. After midnight, there was a knock at the door. Mom hurried to open it. It was a man from the mine.

"Mrs. Anderson. There's been an accident. Your husband's hurt pretty bad. He went by ambulance to the hospital. I'm sorry!"

Mom hurried to wake Sonny, who had recently received his driver's license.

"Hurry, son! Get up! Your daddy's been hurt in the mine. We have to go to the hospital now!"

MOM AND DAD

Sonny got dressed in a hurry, and the two hurried to St. Mary's Hospital in McAlester. Marilyn, Phyllis, and I remained home to await the outcome. We soon learned of Dad's injuries, a broken collar bone, most of the ribs broken on one side, and three or four on the other side. He also suffered internal injuries, and all injuries were life-threatening. Shortly after he had gone to work that night, he was crossing a large conveyor belt when his foot got caught underneath. He was pulled beneath the conveyor, and was rolled along, crushing his ribs. Soon, a co-worker saw what was happening, and turned off the switch to the conveyor. He related that Dad's helmet had gotten stuck in the conveyor, and the strap was also choking him. He managed to free him from this, and summon other workers to extricate him from the conveyor. He was sent to the surface where an ambulance awaited his transport to the hospital. It was a horrible night for us all. We almost lost our dear dad on that night.

Dad had a dear friend at this time, L. C. Duff. They were best pals, hunting and fishing together, and consuming a lot of choc beer. The morning following the accident, L. C. was there. He helped to scrub the oil and tar from Dad's body, even washing his hair to remove the scum. He was crying, and begging Dad to not return to the mine. During those times, there was no orthopedic surgeon as such. He was treated by Dr. E. H. Shuller, who had some skills in this area. He wrapped Dad's rib cage the best he could, and pinned his collarbone. Years later there was a large bump where the pin was placed. For many months, Dad was so sore that if he sneezed or coughed, it brought tears to his eyes. His greatest pain, however, came from his inability to provide for his family for some time. He was soon out in his garden, though, doing his utmost to raise the delicious vegetables. We survived on these, as well as well-fed chickens, and Mom's home-made bread. Dad was too proud to take any hand-outs, or charity from others. After about a year, while still recuperating, he took a job at a laundromat in McAlester, cleaning and doing maintenance work on the machines. After some more time passed, and he grew stronger, he went to work at the Army Ammunition Plant at Savanna, Oklahoma. Here he remained until his retirement some years later. Dad never had a great deal of formal education, but he did quite well in his retirement years. At this time, he was drawing his social security, black lung from the coal mine years, and a check from his retirement from the army base. He managed to put away a sizeable amount of funds for Mom's care after he passed.

In the year 1965, at the age of 21, I had the opportunity to take a grand vacation. I was driving a 1960 black Volkswagen Bug. It was a three-day trip to Oakley, California, to visit my uncles, aunts, and cousins. It was quite an adventure, driving that little Bug across the endless desert toward Bakersfield. Half-way through the desert, it began to heat up badly. These Bugs had no radiator, and were air-cooled with a large fan. I stopped to inspect. The belt was ok, the fan was working properly, yet it continued to run really hot. I could not discover the problem. When I crippled it into Bakersfield, I found the nearest VW dealer. A mechanic came out and asked what the problem was.

"This damn thing keeps heating up, and I can't figure out why." I responded.

MOM AND DAD

He reached behind the fan with both hands, and retrieved a large sheet of newspaper.

"I think this is your problem, son. She should run fine now."

He didn't even charge me. I felt like a fool.

I continued on my journey, reaching Oakley in the middle of the night. No g p s in those days. No one knew I was coming. It was a total surprise. I found a pay phone and rang Uncle Smokey's number. A sleepy Aunt Ruby answered.

"Hello! Who's this calling at this hour of the night?"

"Hey! It's your nephew, Bill, all the way from Oklahoma!"

"Where are you?"

"I'm in Oakley, but I have no idea where your house is."

"Just tell me where you are. I'll come to get you."

I explained my location the best I could, and soon Aunt Ruby drove up. She gave me a bear hug and led me to their house.

(Aunt Ruby and her bear hug, October, 1965)

Aunt Ruby and Uncle Smoky married when she was only 14 or 15 years old. I heard many exciting stories about their marriage through the years. There were differences of opinions, and squabbles, but genuine love filled in the gaps. When Aunt Ruby felt as though Uncle Smoky had had his fill of whiskey and beer, she would hide his car keys to prevent him from making a trip into town for a re-supply. He would disrupt everything in the house, and not finding the keys, he resorted to drastic measures. Dad related an incident once where his brother broke every window in the car, and finally hot-wired it, and drove the window-less car into town to buy more beer. Dad was living there at the time, and when Aunt Ruby asked him to intervene, he gave an attempt to calm his brother.

Uncle Smoky turned to him, fist drawn back. "I don't give a damn if you're my brother or not. I'll knock you on your ass!"

"It's your life. Kill yourself, if you want to!" Dad yelled, as he drove away.

Through this volatile type of relationship, three sons were born......Jay, Bill, and Don. As the boys grew up, if Aunt Ruby felt they had had enough to drink, they were not permitted to leave the house. She had a unique way of preventing them. She wrestled them to the floor, and sat upon them until they went to sleep. There was no faking it either!

During my visit in 1965, Jay was a sort of overseer. He was the oldest son, and when trouble was brewing, Aunt Ruby would call him, since he lived nearby. One evening during my visit, Uncle Smoky and I had consumed several beers. Uncle Smoky wanted

MOM AND DAD

us to have one more for a night-cap. Aunt Ruby stood in front of the refrigerator.

"You've had enough! I'll call Jay!"

Uncle Smoky stood his ground. "Go ahead and call Jay. I don't give a damn. Bill and I are going to have one more for the night!"

Finally, Aunt ruby moved away. Uncle Smoky opened the door and handed each of us a beer. I didn't know whether to drink it or not, until Uncle Smoky nodded his head 'yes'. Then we gulped down our night-caps.

(Here we all are! Back row, left to right, me, Uncle Smoky, and Jay. Front row, left to right...Uncle Gene, Don, and Bill. Most of us are holding a beer.)

Uncle Gene was a great San Francisco Giants fan, and so while there, he took me to a couple of games. Of course, we had our beer and peanuts. Uncle Gene was always of a pleasant nature, forever smiling and happy. When I made my trip, I arrived late, so it was the next morning before I was taken to his house. He worked nights in a paper mill. Aunt Dixie answered the door with a look of surprise.

"Oh, my gosh! Wait until Gene sees you! He's going to be surprised. He's still sleeping, but I'm going to wake him up."

Uncle Gene emerged from the bedroom, rubbing the sleep from his eyes. He rubbed them again, and looked at me.

"Well, I'll be damned! You finally came to California. I can't believe my eyes." He rubbed them again.

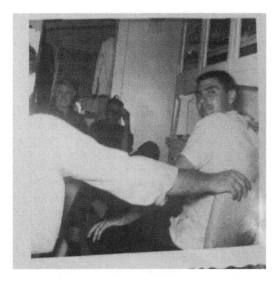

(Here we are again, me looking back, Uncle Gene on left, Uncle Smoky on right. I have no idea whose arm is on my chair, probably that of Jay. Oct, 1965.)

All in all, it was a pleasurable and memorable trip to California, and soon I was on my way back to Krebs in the old VW. There was no over-heating this time, but it was still a 3-day trip. Motel rates in those days usually ranged between 15 to 20 dollars a night. I returned many years later to attend the funerals of Uncle Smokey and Uncle Gene. Dad accompanied me to Uncle Smokey's funeral. It was the first time either of us flew. So, that too, was an adventure.

CHAPTER 11   208

FINAL YEARS

(Above daughter Carolyn poses with her grandparents, Mom and Dad, in their living room. They were in their 80's here.)

Years in the coal mine, and advancing years, began to take their toll on Dad. He became thin, and began to deteriorate physically and mentally. His posture was stooped, and his hips and knees began to give out. He walked with difficulty, sometimes using a cane, only when Mom insisted. His pain was always evident, although he did not complain much. One of his hips eventually deteriorated to virtually bone-on-bone. We knew it was time for a replacement, but Dad always protested.

"By God! I'm not doing that until I can't walk at all!"

Eventually it happened. We virtually had to load him into our Ford Aerostar Van and cart him off to the hospital. Dr. Patrick Gannon, an orthopedic surgeon, performed the hip-replacement surgery on Dad. While he was in surgery, Mom, myself, and other family members gathered in his room, and prayed the rosary for his successful surgery and recovery. He came through the surgery fine, and spent some months recovering.

Soon, he was up and about, using his quad cane for support. The gardening that he loved now was a thing of the past. My brother, Sonny, lived across the street, and under Dad's supervision, he planted a few vegetables in his garden for his observation and care.

A couple of years following his surgery, Dad's mind began to fail. He consistently drove Mom to Mass on Sunday mornings, and would pick her up later. He would often drive to Kentucky Fried Chicken after dropping her off. He always brought home a large bucket, for there were always visitors in the afternoon. Sometimes Dad would not arrive at church to pick up mom, so she walked home. He would arrive later with no chicken.

"What's the matter?" Mom asked. "Are they out of chicken?"

"Oh, hell no! They must have moved the place. I couldn't find it!"

This became more and more frequent, and we began to realize that Dad was getting lost. We discussed among ourselves what could be done. Should we try and take his keys from him? Or try to limit his driving? We knew of his stubbornness, and his independence, and we decided to allow him to continue driving for a time.

Then came one cold winter day in the year 2000. In the afternoon, Dad decided to make a trip to the store. It was around 2 in the afternoon. Mom waited anxiously for his return. When he left to make his trips to the store, he always flashed a radiant smile to her.

"I'll be back before the rain comes."

The rain didn't come that day; neither did Dad. Around 6 pm there was a phone call. Dad had stopped at Ashland, some distance west of Savanna, to ask for directions to Krebs. The gentleman had the presence of mind to know that something was not right. He contacted us and told us of the situation. Hopefully, we thought, dad would locate 69 highway and head for Krebs. We gathered at Mom's and waited. A couple of more hours passed. No Dad. Around 8:30 pm, we decided to try to locate him. We all went in different directions for an hour or more. Still no Dad. We returned to Mom's house to await any news. Finally, around 11 pm, the phone rang. A gentleman on the other end described what had happened. Dad had driven some miles east of Hartshorne near highway 2, and apparently fell asleep. The man described how he and his wife were heading back home which was located in that area. Suddenly they noticed lights shining up in the trees, from a deep ravine. The man knew something was wrong. He exited his vehicle and descended the steep embankment. He located Dad's truck, which was up-side-down in the ravine. Dad was hanging up-side-down, luckily his seat belt was fastened. The man helped Dad from the truck and called an ambulance. He related that Dad was on his way to the hospital, but he didn't think he was severely injured.

We all rushed to the E.R. and located him. He was happy to see his family, but had no recollection of what happened. The only injury was a small laceration on his head which was soon stitched up and antibiotic applied. He was extremely dehydrated, and drank a couple of 7 ups in our presence. He was placed in observation for a couple of days just in case. Mom had not gone with us to the ER, but was anxious for a visit the next morning.

When asked by the nurses what had happened to him, he gave his answer.

"I was banged up in the damn coal mine."

He was going back many years in time, another indication that he did not recollect the accident.

He was escorted down the hall in a wheel chair to meet us. When he caught a glimpse of mom, his face suddenly lit up with joy. Here was his beloved Mary.

In a few days, Dad was brought home, but he never drove again. Even though he didn't recall the accident, he himself knew his driving days were over.

He would look at us. "I don't have a truck anymore."

Marilyn or Phyllis continued going to the store for him to do the grocery shopping, and taking him to Alamo Liquor to buy his wine and beer. He always wanted to be sure that he had wine on hand for Connie when we visited. His hospitality never waned, even in his last days. Should he be napping in his recliner, and awaken to find some of us there, his response was always the same.

"Hey, get you a beer out of the fridge!"

In the hospital following his accident, his mind began to fail more, and he thought he was at home. On one of our visits, he awakened to find us standing near his bed. He looked at our son, Jonathan.

"Hey, Jonathan! Get something to drink."

Jonathan only smiled back at him.

Dad continued to decline in his final months. He became more confused, and developed congestive heart failure. His ankles became swollen, to where they resembled small footballs. And yet, he still managed to wander from his recliner to the kitchen. In the final month or so, he became incontinent, and had to wear depends. He searched for things in the house, not knowing what he was looking for. On one of my visits, he slowly rose from his recliner, and made his way to a lamp stand. He began to shuffle things around.

"Dad, what are you looking for?" I asked.

He gave me a puzzled look. "Hell, that's the problem! I don't know!"

FINAL YEARS

Even in his condition, he maintained his sense of humor.

It was quite amusing, however, when he began to accuse Mom of drinking, or hiding his choc beer. She never took a sip in her life. Mom also was quite a talker, particularly in these later years. Dad would open his mouth to say something, and mom would butt in. Finally, Dad got a word in.

"I"ll be damn! She talks with both hands and feet, and I still can't understand her."

Everyone burst out in laughter.

Dad survived for about six months following his accident. He spent most of his time in his arm chair, watching television and napping. He was always neat and clean, but during these final days, he could no longer bathe himself. His weight dwindled down to around 85 pounds. Because of a pungent odor, we suspected that he may have also been afflicted with colon cancer. He began to twist around in his chair, and grimace in pain. My wife, Connie, a nurse, suspected that he may have some ulcers on his buttocks. He was always a very private person, especially when it came to inspecting this area of his body. None of us dared ask him to investigate, except Connie. He had a deep love and respect for her, and she him. One evening she knelt by his arm chair.

"Why don't you let me take a look at you, and see what's going on?"

He gave her a loving smile. "Well, hell! I guess I'm going to have to do something."

FINAL YEARS

Jonathan and I carried him into the bathroom where Connie could inspect the problem. She soon found some large decubitus ulcers which she treated and bandaged for him. After this, she was allowed to be his nurse for the duration of his life.

The final day of Dad's life came on May 2, 2001. He went out in style. With his football size ankles, he managed to get to the refrigerator during the night, and retrieve a beer. It was found in his lap. At the age of 85, he departed to be joined with his loved ones, especially a mother he never had the opportunity to know. I'm sure the choc and wine are still flowing freely.

Dad was laid to his final rest at St. Joseph's Catholic Cemetery in north McAlester on May 7, 2001. As we all bid our 'farewells', Mom wiped the tears from her eyes, and sobbed.

"I love you, Chester. I'll miss you so much. I'll join you soon, but I don't know when."

We later gathered upon Anderson Hill with Mom. We shared our memories of Dad. Other guests and friends also joined us, offering their consolation. We did not want to leave Mom alone until we felt she would be alright. Phyllis and Marilyn insisted on spending a few nights with her in the home. Finally, she stood her ground. After about the third day, she spoke her mind.

"You girls need to go back home to your families! I have to get used to being here alone. You can visit any time you want."

Reluctantly, they went back to their homes, but we all checked on Mom every day. We had promised Dad that we would care for her. After he was assured of this, he slipped away. Phyllis and

Marilyn carried her to her numerous doctor's appointments, and bought her groceries. Sonny cared for any needs or repairs around her house. I, too, did whatever I could to help. During these, her declining years, Mom agonized over not being able to attend Sunday Mass any longer. She was unstable and feared that she might fall. I assured her that I felt God would understand. She prayed continually, including her devotion to the Rosary three or four times a day. I expressed my concern to her one day about her being alone in the house. She turned to me.

"Son, I'm never alone. Jesus and Mary are always with me."

That gave me the assurance I needed. We did, however, procure for her an emergency call button later on, just in case she would fall, or become sick during the night. Reluctantly, she finally agreed to this. She felt a little safer in the idea that all she needed do was push a button. The button would also alert Phyllis, or one of we other siblings, as well as the ambulance service. One late night, I received a frantic call from Phyllis,

"Mom's alarm button went off! Something must be wrong. I'm going to pick you up. We need to go up there."

Phyllis soon picked me up and drove up to Mom's. She had a key to the back door. We entered the house and went into Mom's bedroom. She was on the bed, but we couldn't determine if she was alright or not. Phyllis shook her.

"Mama! Mama! Are you alright?"

Mom sprang straight up in bed, her eyes wide in fear.

"Who is it? Are you robbers? I don't have any money in the house!"

It was a while before we convinced Mom that we were there checking on her, that her emergency call button had been triggered. What happened, we presumed, was that she had rolled over on the button, thereby triggering the alarm. We apologized to her, and made our way back home.

Mom continued to miss Dad intensely, as time went on. She was often in tears, relating how she dreamed of him, and thought of him constantly. She continued to have deep devotion to our Lord, and the blessed Mother, praying continually. One night about two years after his death, it was very stormy. I knew of Mom's on-going fear of storms, so early the next morning I decided I'd best pay her a visit. Again, she was in tears. I tried to console her, but it was to no avail this morning.

"I dreamed of your father last night, but I think it was more than a dream!"

"Tell me about it." I said.

"I was in my bed during the storm, praying the rosary, when suddenly your Father came into the room."

Her eyes lit up with excitement. "He told me that he could only stay for a little while. And, soon, he would have to leave."

Her eyes became saddened once again, as she thought of his departure. I have always felt that because of Mom's strong faith, and devotion to our Blessed Mother, she was indeed visited by

Dad. He came to reassure her that he was alright, plus he knew of her great fear of storms. Did she see a vision? Or, was she truly visited by her beloved? Again, time will tell.

I, too, believe that we are sometimes visited by loved ones who have gone on before us, though perhaps, not in such a dramatic way as Mom experienced. For me, it often comes in dreams. An example. Sometime after Dad passed, I had a dream. He was laughing, dancing around in the kitchen, and playing a fiddle. Dad never played a musical instrument, and was not much of a dancer. However, I took this dream to mean that he was very happy in heaven with those who preceded him.

Anderson Hill was still our visiting place on Sunday afternoons, where we would visit Mom and take her something to eat. When spaghetti dinners were held at the parish hall, we always brought her a dish of spaghetti and meat balls. She would eat some of it, but would always have something to say.

"This is pretty good, but not like I make!"

I have to admit, she was right. Nothing could duplicate her cooking, especially Italian dishes.

Mom continued in her bossy nature at times. Shortly after Dad passed, she wanted his arm chair moved out of the house. Because of his incontinence, and the decubitus ulcers, the chair had begun to wreak of an unpleasant odor. She approached Sonny and I on one of our visits.

(Mom, Dad, me, and Connie, at St. Joseph's Church in 1995. I was in 2nd year of Diaconate training, being installed as lector.)

"I want you boys to take that chair outside right now! I want it out of here!"

We obliged mom, carrying it outdoors for a time until it could be hauled away. I don't know if it was the odor, or the absence of Dad which bothered Mom the most. At any rate, when she wanted something done, it got done. In similar fashion, a window shutter had fallen from one of the windows on the south side of the house. My brother Sonny and I were standing in the yard when the living room door opened. There stood Mom.

"You boys, put that shutter back by the window!"

Again, we obliged her.

(Mom, and son, Jonathan, May 10. 2008. Mom was 93, about a year and a half before her death.)

During the final year or so of her life, Mom continued to decline physically, but her mind remained very sharp. She always remembered any doctors' appointments, and never forgot anyone's birthday, including great-grandchildren. She prayed continually when alone, and still agonized over being unable to attend Mass. I took her Holy Communion on Sundays, and occasionally on other days. This gave her comfort in the fact that she continued to receive this precious sacrament. She continued to miss Dad horribly, and prayed for him every day. And then it happened! One morning toward the end of September, 2009, Mom was up for breakfast. As she turned toward the table, she fell and broke her hip. We later learned from her doctor, that most likely the hip broke causing her to fall. At this age the bones become quite fragile, and can break even while twisting or turning. This is likely what happened to Mom. Fortunately, there was a lady care-giver staying there at the time. She soon alerted Sonny, who lived directly across the street. He hurried over and helped Mom up and to a sofa. Then an ambulance was summoned, which soon arrived and transported her to the hospital. I was summoned and was soon at her bedside. The x-rays confirmed that indeed her hip was broken. She was admitted to the hospital for surgery. We were all concerned that with her age and health problems, if she could even survive a major surgery. The doctor, Patrick Gannon, assured us that the surgery was a must.

"If surgery is not performed, the broken bones will produce a massive infection which will kill her. The hip replacement is an absolute must!"

Reluctantly, we all agreed, and waited anxiously as the surgery was performed. Mom survived the surgery, and after a few days, was released from the hospital and placed in Walnut Grove Living Center. At her age and weakened condition, she was unable to undergo any type of therapy. A couple of days following her surgery, she looked up at me and questioned me.

"Am I bad? Am I going to make it?"

I grasped her hand. "Sure, Mom. It's going to take some time." I lied.

We all knew that her recovery would take a miracle.

Fortunately for Mom, when she left the hospital for the nursing home, her mind began to fail. She thought that she had gone home. We hung familiar items around her bed, including a crucifix or two, and some pictures of grandkids. Her rosary remained always around her neck, or in her hand, where she preferred it to be. When we left her room following a visit, she always gave her instructions.

"Good night! I love you all. Be sure to turn the tv and the lights out before you leave!"

I always thought it a great blessing that God had placed her in this state of mind shortly before calling her home. She never wished to be in a nursing home. However, she required 24- hour care which none of us could provide, especially the nursing care. God continued to extend his blessings to her. She remained in the nursing home for only three weeks before she was called home. We all visited her as often as possible. She continued to recognize all of us, but still thought in her mind that she was in her home. At one of my visits she was frantic.

"What's the matter, Mom?" I asked.

"My rosary! I can't find it!"

"We put it around your neck. When you doze off it falls from your hand to the floor."

"No! No!" She replied. "I want it in my hand!"

I promptly took the rosary from around her neck and placed it into her hand. This quickly calmed her. She felt secure with Jesus and his Mother in her hand, as always.

Near Halloween, October 29, 2009, came Mom's last day on earth. My wife, Connie, was still working at the time, at the hospital, on the early shift, 5 AM. Every morning on her way to work, she would check on Mom. She thought of not going on this morning, but something told her she should check up on Mom. One glimpse of her, and Connie knew the end was near. My cell phone rang.

"Bill, you better come quick! I think your Mom is dying! She is whispering your name."

"I'll be right there!"

I, too, was still working at the time at the McAlester Clinic in McAlester. I hurriedly removed my lab coat, and hopped in the truck. I was at Walnut Grove in no time, and made my way to Mom's bedside. I grasped her hand which clutched her rosary. She gazed up at me with teary glazed eyes.

"Bill." She whispered weakly.

I knelt by her bedside and took my rosary from my pocket. I clasped her hand containing our two rosaries.

"It's OK, Mom. Do you see DAD or grandma coming for you? It's ok to go. We'll be fine."

She gazed up at me weakly, and after a couple of shallow breaths, she closed her eyes and went to join her loved ones. I lay my head on her for a few moments, not able to hold back the tears. At that moment, I felt the Blessed Mother's presence near us. I knew that she had come to escort our Mom to her eternal home.

When I had gained my composure, I phoned my other siblings and informed them of Mom's passing. Later that morning we gathered at Marilyn's house to share memories, have some coffee, and make preliminary funeral arrangements. Very appropriately, Mom's rosary was held on All Saints Day, November 1, 2009. The funeral was held at her home parish, St. Joseph's in Krebs on All Souls Day, November 2. I was blessed to have the strength to do her funeral homily. Mom was blessed to have four priests in attendance, in addition to our pastor, Father Jim Caldwell. There were also a number of deacons in attendance, including cousin James Scarpitti. She had a beautiful send-off. Today she rests in peace alongside our Dad at St. Joseph's Catholic Cemetery in north McAlester.

CHAPTER 11

A BRIEF HISTORY OF ST. JOSEPH'S CATHOLIC CHURCH

The above photo depicts the interior of St. Joseph's. The large white columns support the choir loft. This is the scene depicted when one enters the church from the entrance on the west side. The altar is located on the east side. Tradition has it that the altar be located to the east, toward the rising sun. The tabernacle is located in the center, directly behind the altar. This is where the precious body of our Lord is reserved. A burning candle is

A BRIEF HISTORY

always located near the tabernacle, representing the light of Christ.

During the years 2001 to 2002, St. Joseph's underwent massive reconstruction. The ceiling and walls were re-plastered, new carpet was installed, the pews were refurbished by inmates at the McAlester Penitentiary. Old shingles were removed, and a new metal roof was installed. The large white-washed statues were also restored in their original colors. Our son, Jonathan, a very skilled artist, played a large role in this, refurbishing all of the stations of the cross, the last supper scene at the center of the altar, and a number of the statues. The estimated cost of this venture was around $600,000! The Church today is listed on the Oklahoma Historical Register, and is one of the more beautiful, historical old churches in the Diocese of Tulsa. Hopefully, our ancestors are proud.

If someone is daring enough, something profoundly interesting awaits him in the belfry at St. Joseph's, an inscription on the bell. "My name is Sybil. I am the voice of one crying in the wilderness." And, immediately below this, "Rt. Rev. D. Isidore Robot, Prefect Apostolic of the Indian Territory." Like, John the Baptist, the bell has indeed "cried in the wilderness." For over 100 years, it has summoned its people to Mass, chimed at feasts and joyous occasions, and tolled at countless funerals, among them, Rev. Robot himself in February of 1887.

The first Mass in our area was celebrated by Father Robot in the north McAlester home of Louis Roth. Following the Mass, a collection was taken up for the construction of a church in Krebs. Due to the generosity and hard work of the local immigrants, a simple wooden frame church was completed in 1886, as well as a two-room school which Sisters of Mercy opened in September of that year. The church rested on the same grounds where the present church stands. Unfortunately, it was destroyed by fire on December 13, 1902. Immediately following the fire, construction started again, and the present church was completed in 1903, again due to the hard work and generosity of the people and Father Bernard Murphy, pastor at that time. Most of the parishioners were of Italian descent, immigrants who came to the big coal mining boom in the McAlester area at the turn of the century. Other nationalities were also represented, including people from Germany, France, Belgium, England, Wales, Scotland, Ireland, Lithuania, and Syria. With their meager earnings, they helped finance the new church, and they gave freely of their time, talents, and labor in construction.

The rectory, completed in 1905, is one of the oldest in the diocese, and is undergoing renovation at this time. Many of the furnishings are antique, and have been a part of the rectory for many years.

In the year 1916, St. Joseph's experienced some problems. Times were tough financially, and a large debt ensued. Some parishioners wanted to sell the property to pay the debt. At that time, Theophile Meerschaert, the first Bishop of Oklahoma, closed the church for one month. All church services were suspended until the matter could be resolved. He ultimately solved the problem a month later by incorporating the property and buildings in his name.

A brief history

The present school was built in 1953, and many of us can recall "happy" days there with the Benedictine Sisters. Names like 'Sister Mary Clare', who must have been 100 years old when she taught me! She kept what seemed to us, a '2x4' on her desk, and used it without hesitation! Mass was celebrated at 7:30 each morning, and it became a ritual for me to accompany Sister Mary Clare, who would invariably fall while in-route to the school. Then, there was Sister Mary Patricia, who was deathly afraid of storms. She always posted two of us at the glass doors to look for approaching storms. We soon learned to spot 'tornadic' activity, so that Sister Patricia would dismiss the class. And, who could ever forget Father Walt Remmes? He would box your jaws in a flash if you deserved it. It was the eye twitch we looked for. That's when we knew he was angry. Father Walt was well known for shooting pigeons out of the belfry with his shotgun, usually during classes. He once expelled two classmates and me for 'playing tag' in church, during Mass. After our parents thrashed us good, they went up and pleaded with him. He admitted us back in a couple of days.

In 1965 our church underwent massive renovation to conform to the new ideas of worship inspired the Second Vatican Council. The ancient Latin disappeared, the church was remodeled inside and out, and the altar was pulled forward in order for the priest to face the people during worship, but by some miracle, the communion rail survived. Most of these changes were beneficial. In earlier times, the gates of the communion rail were closed. No one was permitted in the sanctuary but the priest and altar servers. Before Vatican II, communicants approached the communion rail, knelt, and received communion on the tongue.

No precious blood was administered. Today, the gates of the communion rail are opened. Lectors approach the lectern to proclaim the scripture readings. Eucharistic ministers enter the sanctuary to distribute the precious blood of Christ to communicants, and to help distribute the host, the precious body of Christ. In most parishes, deacons are present to proclaim the Gospel, and preach homilies. This change has enriched the expression of our Catholic faith, and has made parishioners exercise a vital role in the celebration of the Eucharist, not feeling so much like spectators.

Today, some of the ancient Latin is returning to certain parts of the Mass. Still, it stirs precious memories within our hearts.

We are graciously blessed at St. Joseph's in Krebs, blessed with one of the oldest Catholic Churches in the diocese, and one of the more beautiful. It stands today as a living testimonial of the faith of its people and the impossible endeavors of men like Father Robot, who built five churches, two schools, founded a monastery, and ministered to 32 Indian tribes, despite his short time, and overwhelming odds. Many times, without a horse or buggy, he trekked the land on foot! Father Bernard Murphy, too, was a dynamic figure. He came to Krebs at the age of 26, and was largely responsible for the building of our present church. He and Father Germanus Guillaume, who came after him, worked with the coal miners, and consoled their families following numerous catastrophic explosions. Many homes were saddened during those days. Many husbands, sons, and fathers,

A brief history

left their families one morning and never returned. Many bodies were never recovered.

Father Louis Sittere, too, is a name that brings back many colorful memories. Once, with a ruptured appendix, he drove himself to the hospital. The hospital was 70 miles! Father Sittere enjoyed a long pastorate in Krebs, 11 years, and was exceeded only by Father John Higgins, who was with us for 14 years!

Without question, St. Joseph's has enjoyed a long and beautiful history. But, its beauty extends beyond the high arched ceiling, the stoic statues, the ancient altars, and the picturesque stained glass windows. Its real beauty resides in the hearts of its people, who breathe life into it. Many fine and holy men and women have graced the grounds of St. Joseph's over the years. May God continue to bless this beautiful church and her people as we embark toward our bicentennial.

A brief history 230

On the previous page is a picture of the chapel at St. Joseph's. This was added on to east side of the church in the mid 1970's. This is where we have our daily Masses, and our hour of adoration on Friday evenings. This chapel was designed and built by Mr. Gene DeFrange, a parishioner who passed several years ago.

(Another view of the chapel, the stained- glass windows facing the east. Stations of the cross are also visible.)

(Above, the rectory, built in 1905. The cost was a grand old sum of $7000! The house still contains many of the old antique furnishings.)

(This creation, known as The Trinity Garden was also designed and built by Gene DeFrange. It is located on the west side of the church property.)

(This antique large cabinet is located in the sacristy, the room where the priest and I vest for Mass. It has been here as long as I can remember, and most likely is part of the original furnishings. Various items, such as chalices, ciboria, and communion hosts are locked inside. In the drawers located at the bottom, are stored stoles, funeral palls, and other necessary garments.)

CHAPTER 12

OUR ANCESTORS AT REST

In this short, pictorial chapter, I will provide, particularly for following generations, locations of burial sites of our ancestors. In this way, I hope to preserve and honor our ancestry for future generations.

Above is pictured the grave site of my parents, Chester and Mary Anderson. Their monument is located in the old St. Joseph

Cemetery in north McAlester. Their graves are located on the east side, near the statue of Christ and the altar.

This cemetery is an historic one, with many old grave sites, even one which contains a mass burial of several coal miners who lost their lives in an explosion in the 1880's.

Above is the statue of Christ and the altar, designed by Gene DeFrange, mentioned earlier. Mom and Dad's graves are located to the right of this monument. On Memorial Day, sometimes, Masses are offered here, weather permitting. The rock patio and benches were also designed by Gene DeFrange, with the help of the St. Joseph's Men's Club of Krebs.

Many of the old grave sites at this cemetery have wrought iron enclosures as shown above. These all date in the late 1800's. Some graves such as these enclose an entire family.

Vandals are also at work, as shown here at left. Isn't there a better way for someone to get their 'kicks'

This alcove once contained a statue of our Blessed Mother, which was also destroyed by vandals. Perhaps St. Joseph needs to post a guard! This alcove is located to the northwest of the cemetery.

The alcove to the right once contained the statue of St. Joseph. It, too, was desecrated. This alcove is located to the northeast of the cemetery. Hopefully, one day these statues can be restored and protected, along with the rest of these cemetery treasures.

Many of the old monuments at St. Joseph's cemetery are in the same condition as the one depicted above. They are covered with algae and other deposits. The inscriptions on the stones are barely legible due to this condition. A good many of the stones are inscribed in Italian and other languages. Hopefully, in the future, they can be cleaned up and the inscriptions high-lighted with artists' brushes and a contrasting color to bring them to life. The circle above probably contained a photo in earlier times.

The above monument marks the resting place of my grandparents, John (Giovanni), and Concetta Scarpitti. He passed in 1962, and she, in 1982. They are buried at Mount Calvary Cemetery, located just east of McAlester, and across from what is now a shopping center, called Tandy Town. They lie at rest on the east side of the cemetery, near a large mausoleum.

Above rests my great grandfather, grandpa John's father, Stefano. He lies next to Grandpa John at Mount Calvary Cemetery. Here lies my grandchildren's great, great, great grandfather! What a treasure for them and their children to know where this monument lies! Like Grandpa John, he also lived to be 72 years old, my age today.

Herman, Uncle Cap, rests next to his parents, Grandpa John and Grandma Concetta. He lived to the age of 52 years, which was considered a ripe old age for a person who was severely retarded. So, these three generations rest along-side one another. I visualize nothing imperfect in heaven, so I believe Uncle Cap possesses all of his mental faculties in his eternal home.

Above is the grave site of my Dad's mother, Margaret Anderson. She lies at rest in the Red Oak Cemetery, located north of Bache, Oklahoma. Dad was only about six months old when she passed, as can be seen on her stone. She has a flat stone, which is located near a large tree at the north end of the cemetery.

Above is Dad's father's grave site. It, also, is located in the Red Oak Cemetery north of Bache, Oklahoma. It is situated at the south entrance of the cemetery, very near the entry. He was 53 years old at the time of his death. This would have made Dad about 14 years old at the time of the loss of his father. Thus, Dad was on his own at an early age. I'm sure this contributed to his self-reliance and independence throughout his life.

This monument is also located in the Red Oak Cemetery near Bache, Oklahoma. It rests near the stone of Dad's father, James Wesley. I'm quite sure that Maud would have been Dad's aunt. I know that during times I visited this cemetery with him, he always cleaned this grave area, and placed flowers near the stone.

CHAPTER 13

KREBS OLD AND NEW

In this final chapter, I will present a brief pictorial history of some old buildings still remaining in Krebs, and some new modern renovations. Some of the old buildings have an interesting history.

This old one-room shack was once occupied by a man named John Homer. His place was located a short distance east of my Grandparents' home. He drove an old 1950 Chevrolet pickup truck. Near his place was the home of Mr. and Mrs. Knight. It was a large old home, which no longer stands today. Mr. Knight did not drive. He was escorted around by Mrs. Knight, who drove a blue 1950 ford sedan. She drove so slowly that often we kids in the neighborhood would pass her by on our bicycles! One cold winter morning I arose to get ready for school. It was approaching daylight. Suddenly, we heard screams coming from down the road. Mrs. Knight was running up and down the road, clad in her night gown, screaming for help. Mr. Knight had suffered a fatal heart attack. Mrs. Knight lived for a few more years alone in the large house, before she, too, was called home.

Above is a very old building, still standing on main street near the post office. At the top of the building were signs which are scarcely legible today. This building will date from around 1905 to 1910. Adjacent to it once stood an old shoe cobbler shop owned by Mario Fenoglio. Here we could have shoes re-soled or new heels put on for around 50 cents. He was a skilled shoe cobbler, not to mention his delicious choc beer! Today, Mario's home is still standing in Krebs. It has been refurbished, and is owned by my cousin, Steve Robert DeFrange and his wife Phyllis.

KREBS OLD AND NEW

Another old building located on main street just north of the one shown on page 246. This building dates back to 1910. Today it serves as a variety store, located on the bottom floor. I don't believe the up-stairs is in use today, but in earlier times it served as a type of lodge.

This old building stands on the property of a Mr. Sylvester DeGiacomo. It is located on Electric Avenue on the west side of Krebs. This old structure has stood since the early 1900's. It most likely served a variety of functions, including storage, baking bread, washing clothes, and brewing choc beer. It may have even served as a storm shelter from time to time.

Sylvester lived in Krebs all of his life. He served in the U. S. Army in World War II. He was born and raised on this property. After his return from the Army, he remained a bachelor, living with his mother. He earned his living by scrapping, collecting iron, copper, aluminum, and whatever else was salvageable. His mother passed many years ago. He, today, is in his upper 90's, and living with a niece in the Oklahoma City area.

This little jewel, I'm sure, once was attached to the outside of the building shown on the previous page. I was fortunate enough to discover it resting inside the open door on the opposite side of the building. I bet those loaves of bread were quite tasty in 1908!

This old out-house rests at the north side of Sylvester's property. I didn't peer inside to see if it was a one-seater, or a two-seater! In my day, I even saw some which were three-seaters! Can you imagine sitting next to two other persons when you did your thing?

The opposite side of the building shown on page 248. The old bake oven was likely located inside. The door, facing north, could be closed to keep out the cold north winds in winter. The stone masons did a good job for this building to still remain standing, and solid after 109 years!

As I mentioned earlier, Sylvester was a junk collector. He could usually provide any old scrap part you might need.

This ancient building is located on Highway 31 at the west end of Krebs. It, also, dates in the early 1900's. In the early to late 1950's, it was Tony Petitti's grocery store. Here, many Krebs citizens bought their groceries, including my dad. Tony would write out a ticket and extend credit to the hard-working coal miners, and others surviving on small wages. When payday came, usually at the end of the month, Mr. Petitti knew he would always be compensated. There were few dishonest people during these times.

At the top of this old building is an inscription, DUCA, 1910. This building had been built by a Mr. Duca in 1910. It was later purchased by Frank Testa, mentioned earlier. Mr. Testa subsequently sold it to Mike Lovera, who operated a grocery store for a number of years. Following the death of Mike and his wife, Madeline, it was taken over by their son, Sammy, who continues to operate the grocery store today. Available here are a variety of Italian food items, many of which are imported from Italy. Sammy also operates his own Italian cheese and sausage factory on site. These products have become recognized and distributed throughout the country. This old store has become recognized nationally, and visitors from various states are frequently seen purchasing food items here.

KREBS OLD AND NEW

These old columns once supported an old building in down-town Krebs. When the building was torn down, Gene DeFrange preserved them. They rest on the St. Joseph Church grounds today.

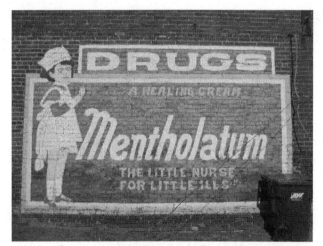

More work of Gene DeFrange includes refurbishing this old advertising sign on the side of one of the old buildings in downtown.

KREBS OLD AND NEW

More of Gene DeFrange's creativity. This gazebo rests on the west side of the Krebs Park. The park includes a hiking trail and a fenced-in baseball diamond with bleachers. In later years, the Annual Terrapin Derby was held near this gazebo. In recent years, it has been discontinued due to a lack of interest, and the protest of Animal Rights Activists. Hopefully, in the future it will be re-instated. It remains a historic tradition of the city of Krebs.

This ring, located near the gazebo, is where the terrapin races took place in recent years.

Above is a large chunk of coal housed in a cage near the ring above.

This tribute, dedicated to Mr. DeFrange, stands near the walking track. This is in honor of his many talented gifts to the city.

The glass doors of the new Police Department building.

Above, the new Krebs Volunteer Fire Department Building.

Dedication plaque on front of Krebs City Hall.

KREBS OLD AND NEW

D.A.V. Building located on main street near post office.

Emblem located on side of D.A.V. Building in down-town Krebs.

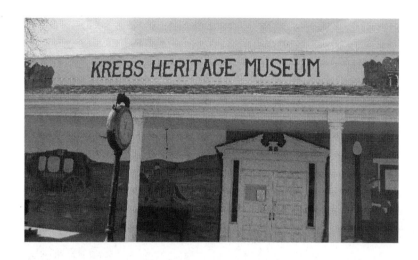

Krebs Museum, located on south main in Krebs, was also designed and built by Gene DeFrange. Many historic military items belonging to him are housed inside.

This painting of a cowboy is located on the outside wall of the museum.

The new Gene Heathcock Community Center is attached to the north side of the museum. Senior citizens' activities are held here, including breakfasts on Wednesday and Friday mornings. Bingos are also held here, as well as music and other activities. Social events such as dancing, and various other programs are also held from time to time.

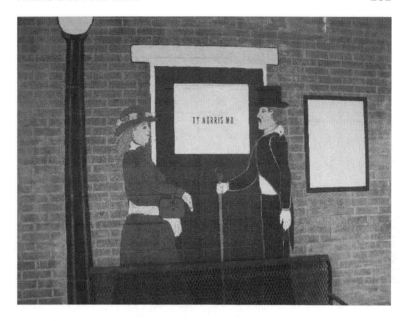

The above painting is located on the outside wall of the museum, to the right of the main entrance.

This car loaded with coal, rests on the left of the entrance of the museum.

The buildings above are pretty much abandoned today, but they hold precious memories for me. On the right was a variety store, owned by a Joe Michael. Here a kid could buy a toy for a dime. In the middle was a small apartment. On the left was a grocery store owned by Steve Tarachione. His mother served as the cashier, and believe me, she counted every penny. Dad would sometimes buy groceries here, but he usually patronized Tony Petitti. With a dime in hand, I would often make the trek to this part of town.

Back in the early to mid-1950's, there were four Italian Eating establishments in the small town of Krebs. Today, three remain, Pete's Place, The Isle of Capri, and Roseanna's. And, they all have a dedicated clientele. They are for the most part family-owned and operated. The Isle of Capri was owned by Dom Giacomo, and opened around 1950. In 1959, he handed the business over to family members, and opened Giacomo's Italian Restaurant on Highway 69 south. I mentioned earlier some of my 'happy' times working there!

Above is pictured the Isle of Capri restaurant, located about two blocks from my home. Delicious Italian food is served here with hospitality. One tradition here, which I've never figured out, is that with each meal a large plate of French fries is provided. It doesn't really fit the Italian tradition, but they are delicious nonetheless.

Above shows the front entrance of Pete's Place, with the inscription 'established 1925. So, Pete's has been here for a very long time. Celebrities come from all around the country to dine at this nationally recognized restaurant. Today it is owned and operated by Joe Prichard, Pete's grandson. Pete's Place had its humble beginning in 1925, when Pete was severely injured in the coal mine. Unable to return to coal mining, he began to sell meals and cold choc beer to starving miners during their lunch break. Today it has blossomed into a large third-generation operation.

At left, a statue of the founder, Pete Prichard himself. He holds in his hand a plate of delicious Italian food.

At right is the choc-brewing factory which has been established at Pete's Place. Various flavors and varieties of choc beer are available to customers, and 12-packs are for sale at the restaurant.

Minnie's Italian Restaurant was in operation in the early 1950's. It was owned and operated by the Silva family. It was situated in an ideal location, at the junction of 31 and 270 Highways. This would have provided a good clientele. The building is no longer functional today. It would require massive renovation, or destruction and rebuilding.

Roseanna's is a family-owned and operated Italian restaurant located on Highway 31 on the east side of Krebs. Many delicious delicacies are available, including spaghetti and meat balls, ravioli, steak and peppers, lasagna, fettuccine alfredo, gnocchi (a delicious Italian dumpling containing potato), and covered with a tasty spaghetti sauce. Steaks and Italian sandwiches are also available. And the list goes on and on. Desserts are also available, including mouth-watering cheese cakes.

Frank Prichard was a brother to Bill Prichard, the father of Joe, who currently operates Pete's place. Frank always had the desire to start his own family-operated restaurant. It was his dream for many years to open an Italian Food carry-out restaurant in the Krebs area. In the year 1975, Frank's dream came true. He, his

KREBS OLD AND NEW

wife, Rose Ann, with the assistance of their children, opened a little take-out restaurant on the west side of Krebs. Frank decided to name the restaurant 'Roseanna's', an Italianized version of his wife's name, and very appropriate.

Frank and Rose Ann on their wedding day, dancing at the old knights of Columbus Lodge, which was located in Krebs. The building no longer stands today. Earlier in the book, I described being at this lodge with my Grandpa John.

After two and one-half years, because of customer demand, a few tables were added in the tiny restaurant for eat-in diners. A few years later, in 1978, Frank underwent heart surgery. Following his operation, and a broken leg, the business shut down. The family was not done. The next year, the family decided to re-establish Frank's dream. They purchased and remodeled an older home located on the east side of Krebs, 205 East Washington. The business continues in operation here today.

KREBS OLD AND NEW

The newly-established Roseanna's Italian Food opened its doors on January 30, 1980. The family worked together to make this dream come true, including many of Frank and Rose Ann's children, and Rose Ann's Mother, Esther (Nana) Morgan.

In the year 1986 Frank expanded the restaurant's seating capacity by adding a dining room on the east side of the building.

Frank Prichard went to his eternal rest in 1988. Rose Anna and the family kept Roseanna's alive and thriving.

In 2006 the family experienced the difficult loss of 'Nana' Esther. Two years later, in 2008, the family lost their dear mom, Rose Ann, and sister Louise. Many of Frank and Rose Ann's children and grandchildren, along with a terrific work staff, have continued the family tradition: Fresh, delicious food, prepared with loving care and pride, for the enjoyment of all of their customers.

Frank and Rose Ann in earlier times.

Made in the USA
Columbia, SC
17 April 2023